D1600373

THE WORDS OF GARDNER TAYLOR

VOLUME 1

The Words of Gardner Taylor

THE WORDS OF GARDNER TAYLOR

VOLUME 1

NBC RADIO SERMONS

1959 – 1970

Gardner C. Taylor

Compiled by Edward L. Taylor

Judson Press

Valley Forge

The Words of Gardner Taylor, Volume 1:
NBC Radio Sermons, 1959–1970
Sermons © 1999 by Gardner C. Taylor
Introduction © 1999 by Edward L. Taylor
All rights reserved.

Bible quotations in this volume are from *The Holy Bible,* King James
Version.

Library of Congress Cataloging-in-Publication Data
Taylor, Gardner C.
    The words of Gardner Taylor / Gardner C. Taylor ; compiled by
Edward L. Taylor.
        p.   cm.
    Includes bibliographical references.
    Contents: v. 1. NBC radio sermons, 1959–1970.
    ISBN 0-8170-1339-3 (hardcover : alk. paper)
    1. Baptists Sermons. 2. Sermons, American.   I. Taylor, Edward L.
II. Title.
BX6452.T39   1999
252'.061 – dc21   99-23027

Printed in the U.S.A.
06   05   04   03   02   01   00
10   9   8   7   6   5   4   3   2

*Dedicated with solemn appreciation
to all who have received so warmly
my attempts to preach the gospel
and to my successor in the Concord pulpit,
Dr. Gary V. Simpson,
my pastor, friend, and, in Christ, my son.*

Contents

PREFACE

This volume contains sermons preached on *National Radio Vespers Hour* and *Art of Living*, carried across America by the National Broadcasting Company.

National Radio Vespers Hour was created by the National Broadcasting Company so that the preaching of Harry Emerson Fosdick might be heard throughout the United States. Ralph Sockman and Paul Scherer, of blessed memory, later appeared as successors to Dr. Fosdick on this broadcast. I was greatly honored, and somewhat terrified, to be asked to follow these illustrious preachers.

These sermons could never have appeared as they are set forth here without the skillful detective work of the Reverend Edward Taylor, who ferreted out the recordings and saw to their being arranged in some orderly fashion. My lady, Phillis Taylor, has undertaken the editing work with a rare dedication and competence.

These sermons are the distillations of my long and happy years in the Concord Baptist Church pulpit. Those, living and dead, who received them with such patience and encouragement were participants in this venture.

"I thank my God upon every remembrance of you" (Philippians 1:3).

GARDNER C. TAYLOR
Brooklyn, New York

ACKNOWLEDGMENTS

I would like to extend my heartfelt thanks to Judson Press for the opportunity to bring these sermons, addresses, lectures, and other works by Dr. Gardner C. Taylor to the American public. The publisher's skill and objectivity have made the process of publication a joy. The technical assistance provided by Mrs. Phillis Taylor, Pamela Owens, Gloria Arvie, and my wife, Constance La Trice Taylor, along with the contributions of DBS transcription services of Princeton, were invaluable.

A debt of gratitude is owed to the Chicago Sunday Evening Club and to the libraries of Union Theological Seminary of Virginia, Yale University, Harvard University, Howard University, The Southern Baptist Theological Seminary, and the Princeton Theological Seminary for the invaluable resources provided to me for the compiling of this work.

In addition, I must acknowledge with appreciation the work of Deacon Bernard Clapp of the Concord Baptist Church of Brooklyn. Deacon Clapp has worked diligently for twenty-five years as head of Dr. Taylor's tape ministry and provided the bulk of the materials found in these volumes.

Most of all I wish to thank Dr. and Mrs. Taylor for their understanding, patience, and cooperation in this project. How grateful I am to have been afforded the opportunity to compile *The Words of Gardner Taylor.* I thank God for having so gifted Dr. Taylor that we should be given this rich corpus of material.

EDWARD TAYLOR

Introduction

GARDNER C. TAYLOR

America's Twentieth-Century Preacher

Early in United States history, the names Cotton Mather, Jonathan Edwards, and George Whitefield begin an exclusive list of American preaching legends. Since then, Henry Ward Beecher, John Jasper, Phillips Brooks, Jarena Lee, C. T. Walker, Lacy Kirk Williams, Sojourner Truth, and Harry Emerson Fosdick are among the names to be added to the roster of those who have displayed excellence in preaching. Many others could be included.

One name, however, deserves singular recognition among Americans who have proclaimed the gospel of Jesus Christ. That name is Gardner Calvin Taylor. Rarely do legends live in their own time, but Dr. Taylor has proved to be an exception to the general rule. His preaching stands as an unparalleled model — indeed a lighthouse — for all who would aspire to preach Jesus.

Gardner Taylor was born on June 18, 1918, in Baton Rouge, Louisiana. His father, Washington Monroe Taylor, pastored one of Louisiana's most prestigious churches, the Mt. Zion Baptist Church, which is registered today in the Baton Rouge Courthouse as the First African Baptist Church.

Washington Monroe Taylor, who also served as vice president at large of the National Baptist Convention, U.S.A., died when Gardner was just thirteen years of age. But under the tutelage of his mother, Selina, young Gardner developed into an outstanding student, eventually enrolling at Leland College, a black Baptist college located in Baker, Louisiana, just ten minutes from Baton Rouge.

As a college student, Dr. Taylor displayed a wide range of interests and talents. He was a star center who led his football team to victory against Grambling. He was a serious student who devoted much of his free time to reading books. He excelled in extracurricular activities, especially debate. Among the several classmates he regularly engaged in informal, friendly debates was H. Beecher Hicks Sr. The debates, accounts of which have found their way into Louisiana Baptist lore, typically focused on matters of faith. Dr. Taylor made use of several resources, but his favorite text was Robert Ingersoll's *The Mistakes of Moses*.

During his college years, Dr. Taylor looked to Leland College President Dr. James Alvin Bacoats, who succeeded Washington Taylor at Mt. Zion, as his primary mentor. Although surrounded and influenced by ministers his whole life, Dr. Taylor did not at first aspire to become one himself. Instead, he wanted to be a lawyer, and in pursuit of that plan he applied to and was accepted at the University of Michigan School of Law.

A tragic personal experience, however, would change not only his plans for law school but also the entire direction of his life. On a spring night in 1937, Dr. Taylor had taken President Bacoats's car on an errand. On a rural highway, a model-T Ford came out of nowhere and crossed his path. The impact was devastating. Two white men were in the car. One died instantly; another died later as a result of the crash. In those days, the society's instincts were to regard a black nineteen-year-old participant in such an accident as a murderer.

Thankfully, however, at the court hearing, white Southern Baptist minister Jesse Sharkey, a witness to the accident, testified that young Taylor was innocent of any wrongdoing. Freed from any fear of prosecution, Dr. Taylor put aside his letter of acceptance to law school and began to think about the ministry instead. Out of this tragic experience, he ended up thanking God and offering himself to God for a lifetime of service.

In the fall of 1937, Dr. Taylor enrolled at Oberlin Graduate School of Theology. While there he wooed and later (in 1940) won the hand of Laura Scott, his first wife, who now sits with Jesus. During those years, the soon-to-be Mrs. Taylor began sharing with Dr. Taylor her love for literature, plays, food, and other elements of the larger culture that would go on to inform Dr. Taylor's preaching. She began her helpful critiques of his work, critiques that would continue throughout her life. During a period in which Dr. Taylor was heavily involved in politics, she said to him, "Your preaching is getting a little thin." That was all the counsel he needed to cut back on his political involvement.

At Oberlin, Dr. Taylor began several practices that, through the years, have greatly influenced his preaching. Most significantly, he immersed himself in the study of preaching as an academic discipline. Like Andrew Blackwood, he realized that every master preacher he respected had made a study of admired preachers.[1] He read sermons constantly, especially those of such nineteenth-century legends as Alexander Maclaren, F. W. Robertson, Frederick Norwood, Leslie Weatherhead, Clarence Macartney, and Charles Spurgeon. He read preaching journals such as *Christian Century Pulpit* from cover to cover.

When a student of preaching inquired of the great expositor Stephen Olford what the difference was between the pastor in England and the pastor in the United States, Olford stated in quick retort, "The pastor in America has an office. The pastor in England has a study." Defying that stereotype, Gardner Taylor has always had a study.

While still a student at Oberlin, Dr. Taylor became pastor of Bethany Baptist Church in Elyria, Ohio. His first pastoral experience, which ended upon his graduation in 1940, affected him deeply and helped him mature in many ways. Since then, he has always shown great love and sensitivity toward those who are starting out in pastorates or going through times of trial in churches across America.

Upon graduating, Dr. Taylor returned to Louisiana to become pastor at Beulah Baptist in New Orleans. In 1943 he returned to Baton Rouge to become pastor of his home church, Mt. Zion. Just a few years later, he was presented with two rare opportunities, remarkable for a man of just twenty-nine.

The first consisted of an invitation to speak at the six-thousand-member Concord Baptist Church in Brooklyn, New York, whose pulpit had been recently vacated by the death of Dr. James Adams. To the astonishment of many, Dr. Taylor declined Concord's invitation to preach because it fell on Communion Sunday at Mt. Zion. (Some would consider it divine providence that on the date on which Dr. Taylor was originally invited to preach, New York City was besieged by a major snow-storm, among its worst ever.) To Dr. Taylor's surprise, he was reinvited to preach at Concord, and this time he accepted. On the Sunday he preached, Concord was filled to capacity. The sermon, "I Must Decrease, and God Must Increase," captivated those in attendance.

The second of twenty-nine-year-old Taylor's remarkable opportunities was the chance to travel to Copenhagen, Denmark, to attend the Baptist World Alliance. On the Sunday morning of the Alliance, he preached at Second Baptist Church of Copenhagen. Upon returning from his six-week trip to Denmark, Taylor was informed that Concord had invited him to become its next pastor.

No one who knew Taylor doubted that he would accept the invitation. They perceived him correctly as a man of vision whose mind was energized with great and inspiring thoughts and who possessed an immeasurable hope and desire to contribute to the advancement of the Christian faith. Many pastors move on because God has placed before them the challenge of a larger church. For Dr. Taylor, it was more than that. His response to this call entailed fulfilling his role in the destiny of the kingdom of God. As Dr. Taylor's friend David Iles put it, "Gardner was big enough for the field, but the field was not big enough for Gardner."

At the 1948 State Convention in Alexandria, Louisiana, Taylor announced his intention to accept the position at Concord. In doing so, he told delegates, "God has called me to preach at the crossroads of the world. I must go." No one in Baton Rouge had to go far to hear Taylor's farewell sermon at Mt. Zion. Radios throughout the black community were tuned to the church's weekly radio program. According to local seniors, it was as if Dr. Taylor were preaching in every home.

At age thirty, Taylor went north, serving the Concord Church from 1948–1990, in the process amassing what is among the most respected pastoral records in the twentieth century. Eleven months into his pastorate, Dr. Taylor began serving on a local school board. He went on to become the second African American to serve on the New York City Board of Education.[2] For a short time, he led the Democratic party in Kings County, America's second most powerful political party organization, behind Mayor Daly's Cook County in Chicago.

Nine thousand people were added during Dr. Taylor's tenure at Concord; the church experienced enormous growth. When the building was destroyed by fire in 1952, Dr. Taylor oversaw the building of its present sanctuary, completed in 1956 at a cost of $1.7 million. He presided over the establishment of the Concord Elementary School, where wife Laura served as principal for thirty-two years at no salary; of the Concord Nursing Home, which was founded with 121 beds, along with a seniors residence; and of the Concord Credit Union that went on to amass assets of $1.8 million. He also helped to establish the Christfund, which was endowed with one million dollars to support community development, especially in the area of youth.

Despite these accomplishments, however, it is Dr. Taylor's record as a preacher that has distinguished him in American Christianity. The diversity and sheer number of places where he has spoken are a measure of the respect he has earned as a preacher. He has preached before the Baptist World Alliance on six occasions. He followed Harry Emerson Fosdick and Ralph Stockman on NBC *National Radio Vespers Hour,* which was broadcast on some 100 radio stations. National denominations from ten foreign countries, including China, England, and South Africa, have invited him as a special guest. He has also appeared before eleven U.S. denominations.

Even as an octogenarian, Dr. Taylor continues to receive acclaim and honor for his homiletic skills. He has received fifteen honorary degrees. He has served as president of the Progressive National Baptist Convention. A countless number of seminaries and colleges have invited him to preach or lecture. Among them is Yale University, where Dr. Taylor delivered the prestigious Lyman Beecher Lectures. Twice, *Ebony* magazine has honored him as one the greatest preachers in American history. *Newsweek* included an account of Baylor University's distinction of Taylor as one of the twelve greatest preachers in the English-speaking world. In an article on the seven great preachers of the pulpit, *Time* called him "the Dean of the nation's Black Preachers."[3]

I once asked Dr. Taylor that all-important question, "Are great preachers born or made?" After considering for a brief moment, he remarked, "I think that God gives one natural gifts, but there are some secrets. Those may be learned."

One of the underlying secrets to Dr. Taylor's success is simply hard work. He has read thousands of books, most of which now rest in his own library. Nearly every week he wrote a full sermon manuscript over a period of several days. Typically finishing on Saturday, he would then commit its contents to memory. Very rarely does he speak without a manuscript of his remarks on file. Given two years' notice before delivering the Lyman Beecher Lectures at Yale University, Dr. Taylor kept up with his regular preaching and writing schedule, teaching appointments, and pastoral and family duties while still finding time to read all of the previously delivered lectures, which numbered about seventy book-length manuscripts.

In Dr. Taylor's preaching can be found a mix that includes a sort of grand nineteenth-century Victorian style, the richness of the African American folk tradition, and a unique interpretation of modern homiletical theory. The richness of his words and sermon design are legendary. Without fail, his introductions whet the listener's appetite. Like *hors d'oeuvres,* they hold us for a time, but make us eager for more. His message moves toward its purpose as a staircase headed to the top floor of a mansion. His rich language, genius for metaphor, and sense of "linguistic keys" help to assure listeners that what may appear to be a steep climb is actually an escalator ride.[4] Each message includes thoughtful theological reflection and biblical scholarship, while steering clear of intellectual arrogance and abstraction. To Dr. Taylor, content and delivery are of equal importance. His delivery contributes to his distinctive interpretation of every text, personifying what Phillips Brooks defined as preaching truth through personality.[5] Dr. Taylor embodies the best of what preachers have been and the hope of what preachers should become.[6]

Hearing Dr. Taylor preach opens a window to the essence of

his soul. There we gain a glimpse of how his character has been wedded to the text. His legendary marking of the cross with his foot grounds him. His thumbs behind his lapels lift him as he hangs his head in sorrow with Job at his narrow window, enters the dressing room while a freshly bruised Jesus puts on his own clothes, or bathes himself in the blood which is a balm in Gilead. Such skill is unique in preaching. He exhibits his own prescription for sermon building, displaying genuine pathos and ethos through his mastery of African American rhetoric, through eloquence, and by grasping each audience's understanding of the human circumstance.[7] These are the very qualities that endeared Dr. Taylor to Martin Luther King Jr. and that should endear him to us as well.[8]

Dr. Taylor has proven the adage that "diamonds are made under pressure." Many people with similar gifts have faltered at accepting the challenge to greatness in their professions, but Dr. Taylor rose to the occasion. Each invitation became for him an opportunity to be gifted by God for the experience at hand. In part because of who he is as a person, Dr. Taylor is revered as a preacher among preachers. His ministry has never been clouded by personal scandal. He has a unique reputation for not changing his preaching schedule when invited to larger or more prestigious places. All this helps to explain why fellow clergy have granted him the standing he so deserves today.

Although retired for nearly a decade, Dr. Taylor still maintains a hectic preaching schedule, frequently crossing the nation with his new bride, Mrs. Phillis Taylor. He recently accepted an appointment as distinguished professor of preaching at New York Theological Seminary.

I am privileged to have had the opportunity to compile *The Words of Gardner Taylor* for the American public and, indeed, for all the world. Most of the sermons in these volumes were first preached in the Concord pulpit. Volume One contains sermons preached on the NBC *Radio Vespers Hour* in 1959, 1969, and 1970. Future volumes will contain additional sermons (many of which have never before been published), lectures, articles, interviews, presentations, and special addresses, including his Baptist World Alliance addresses, the Martin Luther King Jr. memorial sermon, his address at the funeral of Samuel DeWitt Proctor, and the sermon delivered at the inauguration of United States President William Jefferson Clinton.

For half a century, God has used the words of Gardner C. Taylor to shape lives and develop faith. The purpose of these volumes is to help preserve his legacy. The sermons, lectures, and other selections included in this series are far from exhaustive, but they are highly representative. They are intended for readers' enjoyment, but they can also teach and inspire. Of most importance is Dr. Taylor's hope that those who encounter his words, even many years after they were preached, will be drawn to a closer and more intimate walk with God.

Recommended Readings

Susan Bond, "To Hear the Angel's Wings: Apocalyptic Language and the Formation of Moral Community with Reference to the Sermons of Gardner C. Taylor." Ph.D. diss., Vanderbilt Divinity School, 1996.
Gerald Thomas, *African American Preaching: The Contribution of Gardner C. Taylor* (New York: Peter Lang, 1999).

Notes

1. William H. Willimon and Richard Lischer, eds., *The Concise Encyclopedia of Preaching* (Louisville, Ky.: Westminster John Knox, 1995), 37.

2. Clarence Taylor, *The Black Churches of Brooklyn* (New York: Columbia University Press, 1994), 118

3. These remarks may be found in *Ebony* (Sept. 1984; Nov. 1997); *Newsweek* (Mar. 1996); and *Time* (Dec. 31, 1979).

4. Brian K. Blount, *Cultural Interpretation* (Minneapolis: Fortress Press, 1995), 72.

5. Phillips Brooks, *Lectures on Preaching* (New York: E. P. Dutton & Co., 1907), 5.

6. For discussion of the style and content of African American preaching see Albert J. Raboteau, "The Chanted Sermon" in *A Fire in the Bones: Reflections on African-American Religious History* (Boston: Beacon Press, 1995), 141–51; Henry H. Mitchell, *The Recovery*

of Preaching (San Francisco: Harper and Row, 1977), *Black Preaching* (New York: J. B. Lippincott, 1970), and *Celebration and Experience in Preaching* (Nashville: Abingdon Press, 1990); Evans Crawford, *The Hum: Call and Response in African American Preaching* (Nashville: Abingdon Press, 1995); Frank A. Thomas, *They Like to Never Quit Praisin' God* (Cleveland: United Church Press, 1997); Bettye Collier-Thomas, *Daughters of Thunder* (San Francisco: Jossey-Bass, 1998).

7. Gardner C. Taylor, *How Shall They Preach?* (Elgin: Progressive Convention Press, 1977), 65.

8. Richard Lischer, *The Preacher King: Martin Luther King, Jr. and the Word That Moved America* (New York: Oxford University Press, 1995), 50–51.

THE TIME OF THY VISITATION

Luke 19:41–44

He that dwelleth in the secret place of the most High shall abide under the shadow of the Almighty. I will say of the LORD, "He is my refuge and my fortress: my God; in him will I trust."

(Psalm 91:1–2)

Gracious God, our poor flesh is naught but disappearing dust minus thee. Draw nigh unto us, our God, for in thy presence we discover our dignity and our destiny. Breathe upon us the awareness that thou dost dwell with us. Lift us, we beg, into the saving knowledge that we are thy children, made in thy likeness. Grant that realizing this, we might walk the days of our years in service to all who, because thou hast loved them, too, are our brothers; through Jesus Christ our Lord. Amen.

Now and then we come across a passage in a musical score whose haunting, mournful qualities compel in us a sadness and the dropping of a tear or two. Handel's *Messiah* — many of us have been moved to an inexpressible and profound sigh of sorrow when we have heard that aria "He shall feed his flock like a shepherd." Negro slaves, over and over again, captured that mood of infinite sadness mixed with hope which can hang over life now and again. Who can hear "I feel like a motherless child a long way from home" or "Balm in Gilead" without an involuntary feeling of poignancy, almost physical, coursing through his or her entire being? Now and again in literature, we meet passages that stir deep wells of sorrow and lament in us. I never read Bryant's "Thanatopsis" or Tennyson's "In Memoriam" without a strange shiver passing through me. When the whole sweep of human utterance is finished, there is no cry in all the music or literature in the world more loaded with sadness and heavy with lament than

Sermon delivered July 5, 1959.

11

this heartbroken cry of a loving Savior over a lovely city. "And when he drew near and saw the city," says the Bible, "he wept over it, saying, 'Would that even today, you knew the things that make for peace, but now they are hid from your eyes. For the days shall come upon you when your enemies will cast up a bank about you and surround you and hem you in on every side and dash you to the ground. You and your children within you, and they will not leave one stone upon another in you because you did not know the time of your visitation.'"

In this passage, Jesus is bemoaning the rot at the roots of his nation's life and the spent and misspent opportunities of the city of Jerusalem. Here was a city which had everything, so to speak. No city on earth was heir to so much that was uplifting and spiritual as was Jerusalem. A banquet speaker was saying one night that those of us who live in Brooklyn walk among great memories of souls like Henry Beecher and S. Park Catman. True. But very modest by comparison are ours with the memories that gathered around Jerusalem. Through her streets had walked the prophet Isaiah. The lament of Jeremiah was native to its streets and lanes, and the dust of Jerusalem had been dampened by the tears of that weeping seer. There in Jerusalem, David, man after God's own heart, had lived and died.

Here was a city in whose life there should have pulsed the strong things of the Spirit. So many times God had been to Jerusalem. God had walked that city's streets in the national deliverances he had given the city, when heathen enemies had camped at her walls and laid their pagan siege at her very gates. God had been with Jerusalem in all her trials, afflicted in all her afflictions, in the midst of her while the heathen raged. Singers like David had sung God's music in the midst of this city. Prophets there had thought God's thoughts after him. Jerusalem should have echoed down the centuries the cry of Joshua: "But as for me and my house, we will serve the Lord." And yet this great city, blessed of heaven, beautiful for situation, site of the holy temple, witness to the deliverances of the Eternal One, had not known or cared that all of this was gone. The spirit of the people of this city was unmoved and unsensitized toward their God. Blessed with the chance to live in the high places of the Spirit, they chose to dwell in the valleys of small thought and dull living. God had been there, and they neither knew nor cared. Jehovah had knocked at their door, and they never thought to answer. The day of their visitation had been lost on them, and thus the sad cry of Jesus: "because thou knewest not the time of thy visitation."

I wish this nation could realize that God has not given us all this for nothing. Especially ought we to think of our republic on this Independence Day Sunday. America has been visited in so many ways by God. Our natural resources are the envy of the world, and our human resources have come from the ends of the earth. America is a great and worthy dream of human dignity and equality beyond the accidents of race, breed, or birth. America represents in its democratic assumptions a brave new venture in the faith that people of diverse backgrounds and differing creeds can live together in harmony and mutual respect. This, I believe, is a God-given concept which is basic to the American contract with history. How often we have scarred the dream and violated the high destiny to which God has called this land. Now and again, we have gallantly moved forward toward the fulfillment of our destiny as a free, equal society. But we have too often fallen back, as if the destiny were too high for us. In all of these shifting scenes of stress and strain which mark our history, the God of the nations is testing us and sifting us before his judgment seat. He is examining our willingness to test in our commitment to freedom whether, in Mr. Lincoln's words, a nation "so conceived and so dedicated" can long endure. If we but knew the things which belong to our peace.

God, likewise, does come to every life, as well as to the life of the nation. Think you that in your childhood, when you could not fend for yourself, it was mere accident that there were loving hands that cared for you? Behind the care of our parents is the care of another who is also our Father, our heavenly Father, who sees and cares for his own. Behind the food they, our parents, gave us was the food the heavenly Father gives. Behind the clothes they put on our backs and the shelter they provided looms the figure of another who is the giver of every good and perfect gift. Eyes really open can see God in the rising sun that warms our day and in the quiet of twilight preparing us for slumber, in the changing seasons providing variations for our eyes and hearts, in the leaping lightning and in the roaring thunder. Eyes really open can see God when families sit around a casket and give up a loved one to him who has been our dwelling place in all generations. Listening ears can hear God in a little baby's cry, since like as a father pitieth his children, so the Lord pitieth them that fear him. But so often, we fail to see and to hear. Joy comes, and we miss God's presence. Sorrow comes, and we do not see God's mercy in somber garments. So often we miss the day of our visitation. And yet, God is so patient. Hear that lament, like a heartbroken sob in Jesus' words: "If thou hadst known, even thou, at least in this thy day, the things which belong unto thy peace, but now they are hid from thine eyes." Even today, so many missed chances to look up and live. But even today, still there is opportunity.

For some of you, there have been so many times that God has visited and sought you. You bit your lips and froze your hearts and held back by grim determination from his will. And yet he pleads, even today. It is now nearly midnight, the day passes, but even now. You will know what is your problem. Perhaps it is your home that's collapsing around your head, with the sense of family at the very breaking point. You have had many opportunities to make your home good and secure. Many visitations of warning and promise as to how you could do it, and yet you've wasted the green years. But even now, it can happen, and you can know the joy of a home of love and unity. Now, today, in every facet and element of your life, the glow and glory of the visitation of God can belong to you. For God has not quit on you, will not until you've gotten completely deaf to his voice and sightless to his appearing. The days can flash with new meaning, and there can be for you, amidst the decayed corruption of all that has happened, the wild, glad cry that Martha gave to her sister Mary when Lazarus was a long time dead: "The Master is here and calleth for thee." Things are different. The Master is here. So many of you have given up, downgraded your possibilities. And heaven knows, with the mistakes we all have made, it is understandable. We have not known what belongs unto our peace.

The wild, glorious good news of Christ is that even now there can be a new life that soars and sings. It is not too late, not yet, for your God waits, and you have only to strike out on the path where Christ stands out and beckons and bids you trust yourself to him and to what he wants to do in your life. One affirmative nod of your head, one firm yes in his direction, and the wondrous adventures and the far, high places of the Spirit can belong to you. Even today, now.

✑ 2 ✎

A CRY IN DISAPPOINTMENT

Genesis 27

I will lift up mine eyes unto the hills, from whence cometh my help. My help cometh from the LORD, which made heaven and earth. (Psalm 121:1–2)

Our Father and our God, now and again, the issues of our lives seem too much for us. Forgive us our moods of despair that convince us we are marked for unique trials and sorrows. Speak to our faith that it might assert itself. Make us to remember that thou art still our refuge and strength, a very present help in the time of trouble. Send us forth to face our days armed with that faith that we might serve well our day and generation in the cause of truth and justice; through Jesus Christ our Lord. Amen.

"When Life Tumbles In, What Then?" was the title of a sermon which a famous preacher in another land used with his congregation on the Sunday following the sudden death of his wife. In a footnote to that sermon, explaining its inclusion in a volume of his works, the preacher spoke of that message wandering over a great part of the world and indicated that he had received, as he put it, "so pathetically many requests for copies from people in sorrow." What was the secret of that message's wide circulation? It spoke to a need in every human heart.

We long to know what to do in our hour of trial, when dreams have faded and hope is limp. What then? When children have disappointed or a love has grown cold. What then? When health is gone, taking with it the joy of living. What then? Either at one of these points or at some other point, countless people must make their decision as to what they will do, how they will carry it off when the pilgrimage of life moves from an even path to a rocky road beneath leaden skies and amidst gloomy surroundings. In

---

Sermon delivered July 12, 1959.

disappointment's valley, along heartbreak highway, what cry shall we raise?

I want this day to tell you of a man's prayer when life had soured and fouled on him. Esau was a simple, trusting man. He was not at home in the intrigue of drawing rooms or the refined scheming of conference rooms. The Scriptures indicate that he was a man of the outdoors, most at home in the solitude of the forest, stalking his game, exercising his skill beneath the silent skies. As the elder son in Isaac's home, he took for granted that the family holdings would be put in his hands, and simple, honest man that he was, I am sure he would have discharged his trust with fidelity and evenhanded justice. The old familiar account indicates, however, that Esau's mother favored the other child, less physically strong, smooth of skin, gracious in his wiles and charm — Jacob. By the deception of having Jacob, the younger favored son, imitate Esau, the older and less favored son, this mother gained the blessing of Isaac for Jacob. Esau appeared later before his father to receive his rightful blessing. Isaac was dumbfounded, for he had thought Jacob was Esau. His last will and testament, so to speak, had been drawn and executed. He could not recall the act, unwise though he knew it to be. Esau was left out in the cold, so to speak. His rightful inheritance had fallen to another. Out of nowhere, it seemed, Esau's disappointment came, hard and bitter. He should have been the son-in-charge by tribal custom. Now he was left at the mercy of a less honest and less worthy brother. Life had tumbled in for Esau.

For all of us, life does tumble in over and over again. No man, no woman, gets through the living of these years without walking at some time or the other a lonely, deserted way. Life is filled with these interludes of disappointment and sorrow. An acquaintance by a lake one summer reminded me of what a wise man of letters said: "Life is a series of partings." So true! We part from scenes of childhood, from our family roots, from our first friends. Our families are, one by one, parted from us by death. Those we love are parted from us by the demands of life, the call of jobs, the call of the nation. This is life. We plan, and our plans do not work as we hoped they would. Every man, every woman, has disappointments. I have yet to see the human being for whom all plans work on schedule and according to one's wishes. Children disappoint, jobs turn out to be less than we expected, illness comes, misunderstandings rise, friends betray, we fall short of our goals for ourselves.

Some of our disappointments we can understand. Some have come as the inevitable harvest of our foolish planning. Some disappointments come because we are weak or wicked or both. But there are others that are bewildering and apparently senseless. We do not seem to deserve some of the hardships we are forced to face. No matter the reason, every man has his Gethsemane and his Calvary. This note echoes and reechoes in the figures of the Bible. Adam had his moment of weakness and his bitter sentence of expulsion from Eden's pleasant garden. Abraham had his long-deferred hope of Canaan. Isaac had his disappointment of deception by Jacob. Jacob had his disappointment of having to wait seven additional years for Rachel, his wife. Moses had his disappointment of never being able to set his footprint in the land of promise. David knew the disappointment of never seeing the temple rise while he reigned in Israel. Paul, the flaming herald of Calvary's tidings, had his disappointment of some strange and chronic malady. Writers of Mr. Lincoln's life tell of his sadness in the death of a child and the strange mental quirks of his wife, Mary Todd. Every man, every woman, either now or in some decisive tomorrow, must face the shadow of great disappointment.

The spiritual is so true, nor does it refer only to death: "I've got to walk this lonesome valley. Nobody here can walk it for me. I've got to walk it for myself." What will you do? Well, Esau did not run away, cursing his brother, bitter with his father, incensed at his mother. He did not. He went into his father with his sorrow and with his heartbreak. There was no attempt to shield the anguish of his spirit or the tears in his eyes. The Scriptures say that Esau lifted up his voice and wept. I think that there is a place in God's service and among God's children for everything except quitting and turning away. There are days when we must cry out to God, hurt and angry like Job, saying, "I wish I knew where I could find God. I would argue my case before his presence." In disappointment, our cry ought never to be "Well, I won't try any longer."

This is not to say that God does not allow us our hot, fretful moods, when we pound the table before his presence, angry, feeling wronged. It is too much to ask of us an everlastingly calm and gentle spirit, even in our dealings with God. When we rush before his presence, pouring out hot words of resentment, we need not fear that he will not understand. God knows our frame and remembers that we are dust. We can bring any mood before God, so long as we cling to our integrity of soul. When all of this is said, the ultimate cry of higher religion must ever be "though he slay me, yet will I serve him." Even in his moment of bitter disappointment, Esau held on to his love and held on to his belief that his father, Isaac, could bless his soul. There was his bitter lament, surely. There was Esau's raised voice and hurt countenance, yes. But amidst it all was his stubborn, unconquerable faith that his father could still bestow upon his poor, helpless head a mercy that would follow him all the days of his life. There's poignancy and pathos in Esau's cry, but there is also a great triumphant faith as he blurts out his prayer before his father, "Hast thou but one blessing, my father? Bless me, even me also, O my father." I know all of us sometimes feel that desire of our heart has been taken away. There are times in life when the days seem hardly worth living, when the sun has left the sky, and we walk through a grim, gray, cloudy time. But always we must remember that the Lord can still bless us in our sorrow and in our disappointment. He can make bitter waters sweet for us, and he can turn cloudy days sunny. He can turn valleys of sorrow into sunlit paths of joy. This God with whom we deal never leaves and never forsakes. He is always nearby. Our Calvary may be painful and lonely, our course rough and cruel, but God can and will heal our hurts and soothe our sorrows and turn our griefs into glad hosannas. The Judge of all the earth will do right. The desert shall rejoice and blossom as the rose.

The battle is almost won when we can say through the tears, "Bless me still, my Father. The road I must walk is rough and rocky, but thou knowest the way that I take. Bless me in my trouble. Bless me in my sorrow. Bless me in my loneliness. Bless me in my doubts and my trials." And if the desires of our heart are withheld, still must we hold on and hold out and live by the faith that the Lord will not leave, not forsake us. One walking the night with such a faith is sure to come to the morning.

❧ 3 ❧

THE GOD IN US

Genesis 1:26

Behold, I stand at the door, and knock: if any man hear my voice, and open the door, I will come in to him, and will sup with him, and he with me. (Revelation 3:20)

Eternal God, known to us in countless ways and times without number, we turn to thee, that in thy light we might see light. Grant us the mercy of beholding thee in the common rounds and ordinary labors of our days, in order that these poor lives of ours might know the splendor and strength which thou and thou alone can give. Save us, we beg, from pride and prejudice and lead us in thy way; through Jesus Christ our Lord. Amen.

Somebody says there isn't much to people. If you want to look at it that way, that is the truth. We do not live long. Certain dumb animals, I am told, live longer. We are subject to change in our loyalties and are often not too reliable in an emergency. If you want to say there isn't much to people, you can make out a pretty good case. We are excitable and are likely to go plunging off behind the cheap and sensational. We are not very smart, we humans. Phineas T. Barnum made millions off our gullibility and the ease with which we are taken. He said, "A sucker is born every minute." That would account for a lot of foolish, stupid things we all have done. To sum it up — we are so often unreliable.

Our lives are short and sometimes nasty and brutish. We are in heart and mind gullible and stupid, easily taken by slick deals and the absurd notion that we can get something for nothing. That's one side of the picture. You can't laugh or sneer people out of their greatness and goodness on the other side. There is

---

Sermon delivered July 19, 1959.

more than what is low and sleazy and cheap in us. There is something august and splendid and like God. I find much in common, ordinary people that is great and heroic.

Robert Louis Stevenson pictures man as a tiny animal, perched dangerously and briefly on a little island, from which he is quickly and unceremoniously evicted by his irate landlord, death. In spite of his plight, with his frail heart and huge difficulties, man defiantly and gallantly keeps his flag flying, maintaining some kind of decency and honor, and finding time to be kind to others. So we may look at each other with a kind of admiring amazement. There is a great deal of honest friendliness and decency in people around us. They tell the truth more than they lie. They are honest more often than dishonest. They are more often kind than they are mean. There is some of God in each of us.

Langston Hughes has written a novel called *Tambourines to Glory*. Much of it is a caricature of what is cheapest and ugliest in the ghetto, and the main theme of the novel is the description of how people are victimized by racketeers in religion with their pray-for-pay principles, and too much of it is true, though revolting. There is, however, a high peak in the book, where a partner in a new cult in Harlem, touched with the awe and holy aspect of religion, says, "Religion has got no business being made into a gyp game. Whatever part of God is in anybody is not to be played with, and everybody has got a part of God in them."

That's strong language, saying that all people have some God in them, and yet it is exactly what the Bible says. It says that we humans are not just entities that happened, strange characters not in the script of creation's purpose, who just happened to wander on stage. God purposed you in his heart, so that you are not impromptu, something gotten up on the spur of the moment. Something in God ached for your creation and cried out that you and I, and those like us, would come to pass. In the counsels of God's reflection, behind history and before time, God spoke to himself, the Bible suggests, and said, " 'Let us make man in our image, after our likeness.' So God created man in his own image, in the image of God created he him." That should make you stand up a little straighter.

You have wandered off and should take a new direction upon hearing that. We are likely to feel we are so far removed from God that he finds it hard dealing with us, doesn't know how to manage us, can't understand us. Don't ever feel that way. There is in us some of God, no matter how far down we've pushed it, how we've tried to hide it all behind the bed or to sweep it beneath the rug, so to speak. And God still knows about us, no matter how far we've wandered.

There is a striking word in the parable of the prodigal son. You will remember that the boy leaves home, journeys far from the father's house, goes down and down until he is ragged and disheveled. You can almost see the picture of what this princeling has become. A bum in the bowery of Babylon. His clothes are dirty, his hair is long and uncut, his face is dirty and unshaved, his fingernails are unkept, and his skin is filthy and vermin crawl on his body. Not a very pretty picture.

But do you remember what Jesus says? He speaks of the day when that boy, now dirty and disfigured and with the scent of the pig trough in his clothes, started back toward home. When he was a long way off, a tiny speck against the horizon, nothing but a moving mite in the distance, the father saw him and had compassion and ran and fell on his neck and kissed him. The father spoke of this forlorn figure saying, "This is my son!" He recognized him a long way off. This is the gospel, no matter what we have done or where we have wandered.

> Sweet are the memories that come to me,
> faces of loved ones again I see.
> Visions of home where I used to be.
> I will arise and go.
>
> Others have gone who had wandered, too.
> They were forgiven or clothed anew.
> Why should I linger with home in view?
> I will arise and go.
>
> Oh, that I never had gone astray.
> Life was all radiant with hope one day.
> Now all its treasures I've thrown away.
> Yet I'll arise and go.

Something is saying God loves you still,
though you have treated his love so ill.
I must not wait, for the night grows chill.
I will arise and go.

Back to my father and home,
back to my father and home.
I will arise and go
back to my father and home.*

This was the faith of Jesus. He believed that there resided enough of God in us so that what he had to say could reach us. Not that he closed his eyes to what was harsh and base and intractable in us. He knew what was in humanity, the gospel says. He was not fooled into the faith that he had only to start dealing with us and all would come right. He knew the stubborn depths of evil in us, and yet he knew that down beneath the dirt and grime, the crust of hard and great evil, there resided a basic image, the likeness of God. "He came unto his own," the Bible says. There was disappointment, yes, because the God in us is so often submerged beneath so much else. But the power to respond was there. "As many as received him, to them gave he power to become the children of God."

We despair sometimes in this land that the basic best will ever come out in our society. There are things that cut the spirit of all who would be democratic. But the likeness of God is still in us, still in our American society. In Atlanta, during a time of great tension about race, 312 clergymen spoke out for freedom. Catholic bishops and Methodist bishops have stood up to be counted on the side of the angels. The image of God may be marred in our society, but heaven be praised, it is carved deep in the thought and heart of America. There is God in you and me.

Essie in *Tambourines to Glory* was right. There is something of the image of God in all of us. There are strange stirrings and a pull toward the stars in me and in you. There is a part of us we cannot understand, something within us, if only we would listen, that raises up our heads and lifts up our hearts. We are God's own

*Reprinted from *Gospel Pearls* (Sunday School Publishing Board, National Baptist Convention, circa 1920).

children made in his likeness. This is our birthright, and we shall find peace only when we claim it and live by its terms. So seeing and so setting ourselves, the presence of God becomes our desired climate, and we live our days in his sight as if all he bids us see and seek is the fullness of the stature of Christ.

∽ 4 ∾

THIS ABIDETH

Psalm 102:24–28

I said, O my God, take me not away in the midst of my days: thy years are throughout all generations. Of old hast thou laid the foundation of the earth: and the heavens are the work of thy hands. They shall perish, but thou shalt endure: yea, all of them shall wax old like a garment; as a vesture shalt thou change them, and they shall be changed: But thou art the same, and thy years shall have no end. The children of thy servants shall continue, and their seed shall be established before thee. (Psalm 102:24–28)

Eternal God, we are set midst bewildering and frightening changes. Longing for a sense of permanence, we are transient creatures, and the scenes we know today vanish so surely and quickly from our gaze. We need thee as our fixed and abiding center of faith. Help us to remember that thou dost not change, nor is there any variableness in thy judgment and in thy mercy. Set over the days of our years the awareness that on thee we can depend for the vindication of every just cause and the forgiveness of every sin which we, in godly sorrow, bring before thee; through Jesus Christ our Lord. Amen.

A man is musing upon the swift changes of life and upon its impending end. As he reflects, he is reminded that the scenes of life appear and then, like the cool dew before the rising sun, disappear. Perhaps his mind wanders back to childhood, to familiar scenes, the village or town or countryside where he spent his earliest years. They're gone. Memory of those scenes is made sweeter by the widening chasm of the years. Or maybe his thought focuses for a moment on those dear faces and strong characters who sat around the hearth when he was a boy or walked past the house where he played. The elders of the neighborhood who, it seemed then, would always be close by, with their firm expressions, their

---

Sermon delivered August 16, 1959.

26

strong arms and rough hands which could become so tender in comforting childhood heartbreak. Alas, they are gone, he realizes as he shakes his head.

In this frame of mind, a man sets down this living song, realizing that change and time are working their steady erosion and unending decay. Scenes and friends of other days are all passed away, and he himself is marching toward a grave. Maybe as he looks up, he says, "The good earth and large blue sky will remain as fixed points in a constantly changing scene." But then the writer realizes that the earth, which has borne countless generations, is under sentence of decay and death, and the broad, blue blanket of the sky has its rendezvous with change. The heavens shall perish. "They shall wax old like a garment," he says. As a piece of clothing, they shall be put off when worn and threadbare, and he himself, the thinker, was on his way to becoming a corpse. He who mourned at many a grave would soon be the mourned for. Where he had followed funeral processions, others would follow his. Thus, from his pained and saddened heart, there leapt a prayer, quivering in its urgency, trembling in its poignancy: "O my God, take me not away in the midst of my days." Midst all this fluidity, in the very presence of all this change, there was a fixed point, one who would outlast the burning suns and outlive the stainless snows. God is eternal! "Thou art the same," he cried, "and thy years shall have no end," so states Psalm 102. Here in this hope, the psalmist takes his stand.

There are times when we are sharply reminded of the swift shift of life's scenes and circumstances. We meet an old and treasured friend after years of not seeing each other, and an almost painful tug is at the heart upon noting the changes the years have wrought in the countenance of that friend. A fragrance, a sentence in a book, or a picture suddenly reminds us of the dear, dead days that come not back again, and we know again a kind of sweet sorrow in our memories. We are under sentence at the same time to continue moving. There is here no abidingness in the things that are physical. Childhood's gay skip soon becomes maturity's dull trudge. The middle years pass so rapidly into the evening season, when so much of living is a memory of days that were and are no more. All the while, around us there is the increasing number of empty places where once sat those we knew and loved. We think of them and pause a moment with the wistfulness of Tennyson when he wrote, "Oh, for the touch of a vanished hand and the sound of a voice that is still."

Then again, we lament when we read these memorable words from the wise old book: "All flesh is grass. The grass withereth, the flower fadeth." We need midst the flux and change abidingness. The men who go to sea have little that is fixed. You can stand on the deck of an oceangoing ship and you will see water, water all around, as a familiar piece of poetry has it. All the heaving, foaming waves look the same. There is no way in watching the ocean to gauge distance, since there is no fixed point in the never-resting sea by which to measure movement. The skies overhead offer no landmark, save one. The seaman sets his course by the North Star, for midst all the ceaseless, changing turbulence of earth and sky, the North Star remains fixed, and thus he charts his course.

Amidst this restless, rolling, raging sea we call life, is there a North Star, a fixed point in the creation, a constant in the presence of change, an abidingness where all else is decay? Yes, there is one, only one, the psalmist would say. God is here! We must sail life's voyage by his position or become derelicts on the face of a heaving sea. God is the same. He shall endure. "His years have no end," wrote the man. His judgment hangs over our years. Have you ever thought what it would be like to have a God deciding our faith who is subject to change in his view of right and wrong? Deep within us, there pulsates a desire to do right, to be right. I do not believe that any mentally and spiritually healthy person desires to do wrong. There is no pleasure in our transgressions, really. We are in quest of peace and satisfaction, and if our choice of goals is sometimes dreadfully wrong, it is not because we will to be evil. We desire the right. Suppose for a moment that the God who is the umpire of our deeds was shifting and changing in his standards of goodness and evil. What an impossible scramble life would be! Where there are no standing rules, no abiding principles that stand no matter what happens, those who live under such misrule are frustrated, and those who deal with such meaninglessness are rendered helpless and bewildered.

Our American leaders in international relations used to say that one of the key problems in dealing with certain lands was that it had become a cardinal point of a sort of diplomacy to make words mean what the rulers wanted them to mean at any given time. Our moral sense need not be outraged in our dealing with God because while human fads may shift and change, God's laws remain the same. The Ten Commandments are as basic to God's law as they were that fateful day when Moses stood in the trembling, smoking mountain and took dictation from God's own prompting. Mr. Lincoln recognized this when, amidst the smoke and roar of the Civil War, he wrote, "Fondly do we hope, fervently do we pray that this mighty scourge of war may speedily pass away. Yet, if God wills that it continue, until all the wealth piled by the bondmen's 250 years of unrequited toil shall be sunk, and until every drop of blood drawn with the lash shall be paid by another drawn with a sword, as was said 3,000 years ago, so still it must be said that the judgments of the Lord are true and righteous all together." God's judgments abide. God still frowns on deceit and trickery as much as he did the day that Jacob was driven from home by his plot against Esau. God still despises envy as much as he did when he turned his back on Saul or, rather, Saul turned his back on God. He despises our adulteries as much as he did when David let Bathsheba's beauty lead him to stain his honor. Yes, people may change what they call right and wrong, but God's truth abides.

Jesus underscores this when he says, "For truly I say to you, till heaven and earth pass, one jot or one tittle shall in no wise pass from the law until all is accomplished." He makes the scroll of the skies and the rolling hills and level plains the surety, the bond for the abidingness of God's word. God remains the same in the spur he puts on our spirits. We desire to be at ease spiritually as well as physically. We want to stop striving, to quit trying. But God is in our lives, reminding us that we have not yet reached our goal. We have here no abiding city. We are pilgrims and strangers. We are not the saints we ought to be. But every time we bend our knees, and every time we sing the songs of faith, and every time we think about God, a stab of sorrow crosses our hearts. As the lovely hymn has it, "Lord, I long to be perfectly whole." This yearning toward something which we do not quite envision ourselves results in a constantly recurring pain and prodding. We sense, if only by dim surmise, our imperfections. This desire for fulfillment inspires the finest literature and noblest art. It is the universal instinct of people, as if once they occupied some Eden which they have lost and once knew a stature which belongs to them no more. A Negro spiritual put this universal longing of humankind into a plaintive assertion: "Lord, I want to be a Christian in my heart." God is the same in meeting this need. As another psalm says, "Thy mercy is from everlasting to everlasting."

We are strange creatures, setting our hopes and dreams against the apparent facts, or so it seems. We must die, and yet the instinct to live is deep within us. We would protect our loved ones, and yet we are so utterly helpless when they must face physical pain and spiritual torment. Our faith is, at its summit, in the confidence that God abides to give meaning and merit to our days, and because he lives, we shall live also. Here and hereafter, God abideth, our shelter midst the stormy blast and our eternal home. Then every day, let us live in that faith until the evening comes and the busy world is hushed and our work is done. We'll then still forge ahead and leave the rest to God.

☙ 5 ❧

BEHIND THE CLOUD

Psalm 97:2

Clouds and darkness are round about him: righteousness and judgment are the habitation of his throne. (Psalm 97:2)

Faithful and unchanging Father, we walk often with thy face hidden from our view. Our limitation of understanding often veils thy face from us; our weakness and wickedness often distort the clarity with which we would see thee. Forgive us our failure to see thee in our days as thou wouldst have us look upon thee. In the midst of our failures, our God, grant that we may have moments when the veil does lift and the clouds do scatter, and we see thee in the beauty of thy holiness and the holiness of thy beauty. Though our path leads through the night, in remembered light may we walk until the morning comes again; through Jesus Christ our Lord. Amen.

There is in most of us an insatiable desire to want to know the make-up and disposition of those about us. We never stop looking for clues that will indicate to us the nature of the personality of our colleagues in daily work. We probe and search for signs of the emotional equipment of our children. Biographies and autobiographies are read with great interest because we are curious to know what the subject of the biography or the writer of the autobiography is like. When one of our friends meets a figure of celebrated reputation, the persisting question we want to ask about the well-known person is "Well, what is he like?" "Describe her for me," someone asks. We ask this question about God.

The whole burden of the churches in our communities, therefore, is to lead people toward a better understanding of the God with whom we are dealing. For, make no mistake, we are not

---

Sermon delivered August 23, 1959.

in this thing alone. There is someone else who is at work in this world. When Albert Schweitzer began his work in Africa, he went to a certain village and was seeking to convert the chief of that village to the Christian faith. During the course of his conversation, Schweitzer tried to describe the Christian God to the leader of the tribe. After a while the chief cut in on Schweitzer and said, "Yes, we know that at evening when the sky lamps come out there is someone who passes on the edge of the forest, but we never call his name." Many of us never call his name, but there is a God who passes over and over again the places where our lives are cast.

The psalmist says that one of the first things we need to recognize is that this God we serve is not easily understood, and indeed, some ways of his we will never find out about in this life. The psalmist says, "Clouds and darkness are round about him." This singer in Israel is not alone in this conclusion about God. Over and over the seers and prophets of Israel declare unto us that we shall not comprehend the infinity of God in our finite minds. Nor shall we grasp the God of heaven and earth in our little earthbound senses. "For my thoughts are not your thoughts, neither are your ways my ways," saith the Lord. "For as the heavens are higher than the earth, so are my ways higher than your ways, and my thoughts than your thoughts." That's the way the Bible puts it.

The sheer greatness of God reflected in the works of his hands is too much for us to understand. J. D. M. Rourke complained that a fault in the Hebrew biblical genius is the fault of what he called "the tendency to the giantesque." He meant, of course, that the Hebrews spoke in the Bible in such huge terms about God and religious faith that they might be thought to have exaggerated. Such critique must never have sensed the greatness of the God with whom these Hebrew prophets and singers were sure they were dealing. No person could accuse the Hebrews of exaggerating about God if, like them, he had sensed that "the heavens declare the glory of God, and the earth showeth forth his handiwork." We can think great thoughts about God while still recognizing our inability to comprehend him fully, if we ponder carefully that passage, for instance, which speaks of God as the one who has "measured the waters in the hollow of his hand, and meted out heaven with the span, and comprehended the dust of the earth in a measure, and weighed the mountains in scales, and the hills in a balance." This is tremendous language. The sheer hugeness of God's reflection in nature is mysterious. Clouds and darkness are round about him.

We find it difficult and sometimes impossible to understand the ways of God in the affairs of humanity. There is so much evil in the world that seems to go for so long unpunished. We cry out for an understanding that does not come when we go through the almost endless wards of our hospitals and see great numbers of people there. Many of them are those with whom we have worked, helpless now or enduring great pain. Our souls then cry out for some explanation of why God lets these things happen. I, for one, am impatient with the fact that evil is so often in the saddle. I preached to a Jewish congregation during its Friday evening service not long ago. As we went through the ancient, ennobling pageantry of Israel's faith, I thought of their long years of sorrow and slavery. The mind ran to that unspeakably horrible time when a supposedly civilized people suddenly fell back mysteriously and incredibly to a state worse than primitivism and six million Jews were destroyed in Germany. How could this happen in the same world where there is a God? I confess that I do not follow clearly the reason why God allows great numbers of people to be exploited and preyed upon. What have they done that they should go on generation after generation suffering inequities? Their children getting less education, their job status the poorest and most insecure. One cries like the martyrs beneath the altar, "O Lord, how long?"

Sometimes a deeper despair rises like a foggy mist in our swampland of bewilderment and hurt. We wonder if there is a God anywhere. Looking at the sorrow, the pain, the evil, the exploitation, we are sometimes tempted to take the position of a young man in one of Hugh Walpole's novels who says, "You know, you know there can't be a God, Vanessa. In your heart, you must know it. You are a wise woman, you read and think.

Well, then, ask yourself, how can there be a God and life be as it is? If there is one, he ought to be ashamed of himself. That's all I can say." And sometimes, we feel like that. How long before liberty's morning will fully come? How long before the brotherhood of man will be a living truth? How long before truth will stand conqueror over prostrate lie? How far the Promised Land?

Yes, darkness and clouds are around about him. But the psalmist does not stop there. Midst the darkness there is some light. "Clouds and darkness around about thee," but he goes on, "righteousness and judgment are the habitations of thy throne." Hold on now, here is something new. Justice and righteousness dwell around God's throne. The veil of the sanctuary half lifts. The clouds are rolled back now and then. And in the swift rush of events, we can see righteousness and justice sitting as if at home around God's throne. That's a figure of speech to give you pause.

Robert Louis Stevenson said, "If I from my spy hole looking upon a fraction of the universe yet perceive some broken evidences of a plan, shall I be so mad as to complain that all cannot be deciphered?" I think all of us have seen some broken evidences of a plan. Truth seems so weak against lies. It has not maneuverability, can't sidestep and backtrack and change course and shift strategy to suit the expediency of moment. But every lie at last slips, stumbles, and falls down. Truth, on the other hand, crushed to earth rises again. I think I see some broken evidences of a plan. One sees great and cruel nations in history strutting their way to what, according to their swaggering power, seems like a permanence that no accident or design can change. And yet, one looks again for such a nation as, for instance, Hitler's Germany, and it has disappeared. The nations who seemed weaker, surely less dedicated to destructive power, live on. And such a nation, apparently invulnerable, goes down. Righteousness and justice are the habitations of his throne.

I think I see some evidences of a plan. Our lives are blessed in the good earthly things that are beyond our merit. Each time we sit to eat a meal sober reflection will say to us that we are really guests at the table of the Host who could make and grow the grain of the earth and the meat of the forest. That Host would have to be God. There is evidence of a plan, though often broken evidence. I think I see evidence of a plan. Let heaven be thanked for those who feel a mysterious compulsion to enlist on the side of right against all that is unjust and unfair, never mind the odds. It is as if someone nudges us, won't take excuses, and thrusts us forward into the fray. That would have to be God, you see, who has so high a stake in how the struggle issues. We cannot perceive him clearly. Clouds and darkness are around about him. But now and again the mist parts. Now and then the clouds lift. Now and then we see a light piercing the darkness. And in that moment when we behold the ways and works of God, we know all is well, for righteousness and justice are the habitation of his throne. You and I live our days in that confidence.

THE PERFECT INVITATION

Matthew 25:31–46

Come ye, let us go up to the mountain of the LORD, *to the house of the God of Jacob; and he will teach us his ways, and we will walk in his paths. (Isaiah 2:3)*

Eternal God, who alone dost rule the ragings of the sea and whose name is high above every name. We bow in awe and reverence before thee. Even as we bow, help us to remember that thou dost not hold us at a distance, though we are sinners. In all the changing scenes of our lives, help us to bear in mind that we are welcome in thy presence. Give to us the abiding awareness that thou dost bid us to come boldly before thee, bringing all of the conditions and circumstances to which our poor flesh is heir. Help us to live in the sure faith that thy love for us is stronger than all our rebellions, and so win us to thy gracious rule in our lives; through Jesus Christ our Lord. Amen.

Many people think of God as a harsh, frowning figure who sits watching us with grim, disapproving eyes. This is a somber, gloomy reading of life. Many of us are inclined to the belief that life is basically and essentially unkind because we think that God is hard and critical of us. A great deal of this comes from the thinking of the ancient Greeks, who could never come to believe that their gods were kind and friendly. In the ancient account of Prometheus, the Greeks gave their idea of a reluctant God. Prometheus brought the divine fire to earth, but it was not willingly given to humanity. Prometheus had to steal it, and for his act was punished by the angry deities. We speak of stealing a few minutes of peace, stealing a few minutes of happiness. We think that good things are wrested from life and God only by sheer effort and careful scheming.

Sermon delivered August 30, 1959.

Jesus does not support this idea. He does not, of course, close his eyes to the heavy, hard aspect of life. He recognizes the stern demands of crosses and equally the harsh hurt of trouble. "Take thy cross," he says to his disciples. "In the world, ye shall have tribulation," he warns. But with all, Jesus recognized that at its heart, life has a kindness because God is good and kind. He saw everywhere signs of a tender, willing hand of love outstretched, showering blessings upon a world which God has made and in which he maintains final control.

In one of the most searching parables our Lord told, he spoke of both the firmness and tenderness of God's love. It would be wrong to act as if God is only lightness and tenderness. For when Jesus spoke of the final judgments of God, he thought of sheep and goats divided by their own deeds before the judgment seat of Christ. There is a stern word here of which we all had better take full notice. The chilling, final, terrible words are spoken: "Depart from me," he said, "into everlasting fire, prepared for the devil and his angels." But there is also word of infinite tenderness: "Come, ye blessed of my Father, inherit the kingdom prepared for you from the foundation of the world."

So, Jesus says that God gives to us the perfect invitation: "Come, ye blessed of my Father." How can we then think that we must worm our way into God's favor? There was a day when people spoke in awed terms of seeking God, as if he is lost. The Old Testament, with all of its passages of heartrending warmth, sometimes so emphasizes the awe and holiness of God until he becomes a frightening, austere figure. At Sinai's awful tremors, a rope must be strung around the mountain, lest the people coming too close be destroyed. In that overwhelming motion picture The Ten Commandments, the writing of the commandments is an awesome spectacle. A deep, thundering voice, a leaping fire that sizzles the commands of God in the very rock of the mountain. This all makes for an awful, terrible God. "Before Jehovah's awful throne," begins a stately old hymn.

This spirit is true, but it is not the whole truth. In his words "Come, ye blessed of my Father," Jesus is saying that God is willing, anxious. He speaks likewise of God as a patient, loving father in the parable of the prodigal son, or the prodigal father, as it might be entitled. There he refers to the heavenly Father as a tender Father, with a heart full of love. Dare we believe it? "Come nearer," says God, "I want you close. Don't be afraid. You need not cower or cringe around me. Come closer to me." We ought to despise the moods and days in which we have been frightened of God. He loves, he's interested in us. If things are rough with you today, don't you believe that God will ever willingly or spitefully hurt you. Jesus said to parents, "If you, being evil, know how to give gifts to your children, how much more shall your heavenly Father?"

One day a little girl, my daughter Martha, and I stood in the back of a great sanctuary, facing the altar. The lights were out, save on the dossal cloth far at the front, behind the altar. As we stood back in the shadows, this little girl edged closer to me and said, "I'm afraid." I said, "You need not be. This is God's house. Let's walk forward." As we came toward the lighted altar, this little girl said, "I'm not so afraid now as we get closer." Fear ought to fill us when we are far from God. We see, as we get closer to him, not a frown, but a smile on his face. His fists are not clenched as we get closer to him, but are outstretched, welcoming hands. He wants us to come close, to speak before his gracious throne the inmost desirings of our heart. It is not dangerous! It is safe and pleasant close to God. "Beneath the shadow of thy throne, thy saints have dwelt secure. Sufficient is thine arm alone and our defense is sure." "Come, ye blessed of my father." Stand close, believer, it is all right.

"Inherit the kingdom," said Jesus in this perfect invitation. The very word *inherit* calls to our minds a parent who has been thinking about us. We are not aimless drifters wandering here and yonder without a home. We are not ragamuffins or orphans sleeping under bridges or wherever we can steal a night's lodging. We are not orphans scurrying for bread and having to get it solely by our wits. We are our Father's children, and he loves us one and all. We speak of having to make our way, but this is only half a truth. Our way is made for us. We only have to walk in it. God does see about his own. All other apparent evidence is spurious.

All other gloomy conclusion is artificially based. We are not in it alone. We do not have to steal to make our way. We do not have to lie to get ahead. We do not have to scheme to make our way. Inherit!

An old and dear teacher of mine, Francis Buckler, in his clipped Cambridge accent, used to tell us of God's kingdom as the kingdom that cannot be forcibly seized. So no man can flex his muscles and gain God's favor. Likewise, no man need or can batter his way into what God has for him. But a meek and quiet spirit, with eyes and heart wide open to God and hands willing, can get without violence and without fighting all that God has. "Blessed are the meek, for they shall inherit the earth." Oh, how you and I need to hear God saying to us, about our worthiest desires, as he said to Abraham, that man of faith, "Lift up thine eyes and look from the place where thou art northward and southward and eastward and westward, for all the land which thou seest will I give thee." Never let the mood of abandonment own you.

There was a day when Muhammad, with one lone friend, was pursued by his enemies. The case seemed all lost and hopeless. With crestfallen countenance, the friend looked at Muhammad and said, "Alas, we are alone. We are only two of us alone. What can we do?" To which Muhammad replied, "We are not two, we are three, for God is with us, and he means us good."

There is another word at the last, "prepared for you from the foundation of the world." We think that life moves along by chance, happenstance. A fine old psalm has it this way, "O Lord thou knowest my downsitting and mine uprising and understandest my thought afar off." The things the Lord hath in store for us are not chance events, impromptu, gathered on the spur of the moment. The Lord has made provisions. Not this morning, not last year, not last century. But the Lord has provided for our needs from the morning of creation, when as the Bible says in a lovely passage, "The morning stars sang together, and the sons of God shouted for joy."

Can you believe that? Who knows what tomorrow will bring? Some of us will leave this day to face a week of joy. Others will go forth to fiery trials and to the valley of the shadow. But we can all go forth knowing that the Lord has prepared for us. There will be waiting for us, whatever our lot, the mighty hand of God to lead us through. Did you think when you came safely through that hard and difficult way that it was sudden luck that opened a path for you? Nay. It was the Lord. He makes things ready. He spreads the table. He opens the door. He bids us welcome. He opens the path through the roaring sea for his troubled ones. He throws up a highway in the desert for his people. Listen to these strong, calm old words again and take heart: "The Lord is my shepherd, I shall not want. He maketh me to lie down in green pastures. He leadeth me by the still waters. He restoreth my soul. He prepareth a table before me in the presence of mine enemies. He anointeth my head with oil. He maketh my cup to run over." He hath, and he will.

$\backsim 7 \backsim$

THE PROMISE OF RENEWAL

Isaiah 40:31

But they that wait upon the LORD *shall renew their strength; they shall mount up with wings as eagles; they shall run, and not be weary; and they shall walk, and not faint. (Isaiah 40:31)*

Gracious God, thou hast made provisions for our needs far beyond our power to know or tell. We beg that thou wouldst forgive us our fretfulness and the fever of our ways. We act so often as if thou does not care and hast not provided. Lead us into that sanity of the spirit which makes us realize that we walk a way overrun with blessings and bounties. We grow weary and faint at the facing of the issues of our lives. May we realize in such gray moods that thou still dost live and love and that we shall walk again in the sunlight. Send forth evidences of thy care to those who today sit in the shadow of great sorrow or who are bound in the slavery of spiritual or political oppression. Lift us, lead us toward the high places where thou wouldst have us stand; through Jesus Christ our Lord. Amen.

Always people have believed that their physical and spiritual strength can be renewed. Out of their faith in fresh starts have grown many enchanting legends. Every schoolchild learns of the legend of Ponce de Leon's fountain of youth, believed to be somewhere in the balmy clime of the Florida Everglades. The water rushing from this fountain was supposed to erase the wrinkles of the years, to take from the footsteps the heaviness of the weight of many winters, and to restore the vitality of youthful energy. Of course, we know that this lovely legend is only the fine-spun fancy of human hopes, no matter how wistfully we might wish that the dear, dead days of youth's bright freshness might once again be given to us. We cannot turn the clock back. One of the most pathetic, if not tragic, things in the world is to see someone trying to

---

Sermon delivered September 6, 1959.

erase the deep scorings of the years, either by clothes, cosmetics, or choosing a new marriage companion. There is renewal, but it is not in these vain imaginings.

The fortieth chapter of the brave lyric which we call the book of Isaiah is one of the symphonies scattered here and yonder through this huge, blessed old book we call the Bible. Rarely does one come across an extended passage where there is music and might, beauty and bravery, poetry and power, so perfectly blended as in the fortieth chapter of Isaiah. It begins, "Comfort ye, comfort ye my people." (Handel has taken almost this entire chapter and set it to the glad thunders and gentle sighings of his oratorio, *Messiah*.) At the end of the chapter, like a tremendous climax, are these words: "They that wait upon the LORD shall renew their strength; they shall mount up with wings as eagles; they shall run, and not be weary; and they shall walk, and not faint."

The promise is that we shall "mount up with wings as eagles." "We shall run and not be weary." We need moments of ecstatic happiness. Life cannot be lived forever in the valley, nor should we feel suspicious or guilty in the high days of joy, when all the world's a song and our hearts are filled and thrilled with an unutterable gladness. God gives these great seasons. We ought to taste such moments to the full. A marriage altar, the first time one looks at life begun again in a baby, those high days in the temple when heaven crowns the mercy seat, and countless other experiences of hours lifted above the humdrum of living. God promises that we shall mount up like eagles, sometimes to the upper pure air where sense and sorrow molest no more. These moments, if we allow the glory of God to shine on them, can be profoundly religious in their significance, giving a sanctity to events and experiences that we are quite likely to think of as being apart from God, gifts separated from the giver of every good and perfect gift.

There is another promise. "They shall run, and not be weary." We cannot forever live in these rare and luminous moments when all the world's a song. The tempo must recede, for we cannot survive for too long the times of pure ecstasy. There is a variation which God provides, a variation comparable to the steady gladness of old lovers for whom the first ecstasies have passed. We are not expected to be forever in a kind of breathless, wide-eyed splendor. We cannot be on the wing always. But we are promised the power "to run and not be weary." Sooner or later, we discover that the holiday has passed and that we must return to a slower pace, a quieter round of duties. We must return to the common duties, and how less exciting they can be. As much as we need ecstatic glories and radiant experiences, we need some power to hold us when life is not so exciting. I think the great heroes of any church and any community are not those whose names show in public print and who move from one exciting event to another, but those people, unsung and unheralded, who do the little-praised work in homes and schools and churches and neighborhoods. There comes a time, however, when weariness sets in, and even they need a power to keep them going. Praise God, here it is.

"They shall walk, and not faint." Here is the promise that along the hard, dusty road, when loads grow heavy and there's a dull sameness to every scene, power can belong to us not to give up, not to faint. We need strength for the long pull. In our earlier years we are convinced that the world is our cup of tea. It was made for us, and we were made for it. Someone has told of a class of college freshmen on freshmen day at a Midwestern college, carrying a huge banner at the head of the procession which said: "This college has waited one hundred years for us." We feel that way in the morning years, but then comes the long pull. We discover that the competition for what we call success is keen. There are others who seem to have more to offer than we have. Early ideals seem rather heavy loads to carry when morning wears toward noontime. William Wordsworth, with his genius for the tenderest cadences of the language, set the thought to living meter when he wrote: "Heaven lies about us in our infancy. At length, the man perceives it die away and fade into the light of common day." So much of our trudging is in "the light of common day," where there is weariness, sweat, and hopes long deferred and youthful dreams that turned to dust in our hands. There is no more relevant promise God has made than this word to those who walk the ways of monotony and dullness: "They shall walk, and not faint." The condition of the gift of these powers is a willingness to wait on the tides of God to bear us up and out on brave and glorious voyages.

Someone young of years and hard of heart immediately cries out, "This is exactly what I do not like about all this babbling of religion. I want to be doing things, not waiting." Our land, burdened by the ugly weight of its discouraging discriminations, needs bold action from fearless people who will cut it loose from its old chains. "We've waited too long already" some say. Ah, and thinking that is to miss the point. The kind of expectant waiting, the kind of exciting tarrying about which the Bible speaks is not the idleness of expecting our dreams to fall full-grown from the skies. Not ever! No, rather is meant that confidence, while toiling, that God will strengthen and hold when our arms grow weary and our footsteps are labored and slow. The kind of waiting the Bible means is that of a beleaguered army, shaken by the fierce assaults of the enemy but fighting still. Fighting, doing what needs to be done, but with one eye glancing toward the hills, sure that reinforcements are already storming to our aid. Waiting while working, or better still, confident and expectant while doing what needs to be done, would better describe the Bible's intention.

This waiting on God to which this passage refers is that kind of laboring in confidence which I used to see in my native clime among farmers. The farmer goes on in a dry and barren season, when the land is parched, still plowing his field and tilling his soil, but with a look now and then toward the skies, sure that the heavens will keep faith with this labor, that the rains will come to water the earth and to nurture the plants. This waiting on God is that of which the psalmist speaks when his soul is rocked by the attacks of his enemies, when he is besieged by those who hate him, and when his soul's gates are being battered by a relentless enemy who presses ever closer to deliver the telling blow, the mortal thrust. "I had fainted unless I had believed to see the Lord in the land of the living."

There are mysterious energies loosed when a soul takes a high road and walks therein, no matter how steep the way becomes or how hot and fretful the journey. It is the testimony of every soul who has dared to live for the purposes of God, whether in places of public notice or in the places of obscurity, that an indescribable strength comes to match the task. So take heart! God is nigh! Keep your aims high! Never mind how long and hot and winding and impossible the way may seem on which you have been called to walk. There is a mercy which will attend your path and a power that will sustain your journey. An oft-hurt people have a song out of their sorrow. A portion of it runs as follows:

> Harder yet may be the fight.
> Right may often yield to might.
> Wickedness awhile may reign.
> Satan's cause may seem to gain.
> There is a God that rules above,
> with hand of power and heart of love.
> If I am right, he'll fight my battle.
> I shall have peace some day.*

Here then is the promise that God will renew and refresh us, strengthen and sustain us, along the road in which he bids us walk. You can make it then, pilgrim, since God is near.

---

*From "Some Day," by Charles A. Tindley. Reprinted in *The New National Baptist Hymnal* (National Baptist Publishing Board, 1977), 225.

∽ 8 ∼

FACE TO FACE WITH FEAR

Mark 3:35–41

The secret of the LORD *is with them that fear him; and he will shew them his covenant. Mine eyes are ever toward the* LORD; *for he shall pluck my feet out of the net. (Psalm 25:14–15)*

Our Father and our God, we hold before thee the fears and hopes of our hearts. We confess that we have not loved and trusted thee as we ought. For naught could make us afraid if our love for thee had been large. Help us to remember that we are not orphans beneath the sky but are our Father's children and all our ways are held in thy care. Give us therefore the glorious liberty of the children of God, heirs of all thou hast and all thou art; through Jesus Christ our Lord. Amen.

Fear continues as one of the strongest instincts known to humanity. To a point, the story of the change from a savage to a civilized person is the story of the banishing of groundless fear. Primitive man's life was surrounded by terrors. He walked every step of his life in the midst of countless fears. There were demons and witches and superstitions. Phenomenally brave in battle, such a man was still a child in his terror of the darkness, terror of his gods, of what other people might do to him by magic or voodoo or what have you. When the wise old book speaks of the fear of the Lord as the beginning of wisdom, it says a great deal and states the profound truth that as the God of heaven and earth enters life, the old primitive fears take flight.

One of the deepest and clearest insights that comes out of the Hebrew Christian faith is that God is not a God of whim and caprice. His character does not dart and shift according to what mood he is in or what incantations some priest makes or what sacrifice is offered before him. In him, meaning God, says

Sermon delivered September 13, 1959.

the Bible, there are no variables or turning or shadow of turning. So, primitive fear and superstition decrease as our Christian commitment increases. A person cannot be an adult believing Christian and hold his faith in magic and the power of people to do to him things by repeating words and getting silly articles from practitioners who traffic in people's ignorance.

Apart from this primitive childish terror, there are many legitimate fears. An assistant city prosecutor in St. Louis said suddenly in the midst of a pleasant luncheon, "I am afraid of atomic death." All of us are, whenever we stop and think about it. H. G. Wells, during most of his life, was an enthusiastic believer in the bright future of humanity on this earth. His last book, however, written after the terrors of Hitler and the introduction of atomic death, was called *Mind at the End of Its Tether*. It was a chronicle of despair about our future on this planet. Fear was its keynote.

In the account of the storm on the Sea of Galilee with Jesus and his disciples aboard ship, we see a perfect example of men dealing wisely with the awful instinct of fear. The Master, so the account runs in the Gospel, is tired and weary from the pulls and demands made on him by the crowds. He seeks retreat for spiritual and physical renewal. Incidentally, we might all learn from Jesus in this regard. We tend to stay too long in the heat and rigors of spiritual struggle without relief and renewal. Or, on the other hand, we are inclined to stay too long on the drill ground, getting ready to serve but never serving. The Master chose to retreat for rest and renewal and to alternate between work and rest. As the boat crossed the waters to Galilee, the calm and placid sea was suddenly a mad and frothing demon, whipped to a frenzy by the wild and savage winds. The Master was asleep in the ship's prow. The disciples were terrified. In their fright, they called upon their teacher to help them.

They chose to bring their fear to Jesus rather than to take some other paths that might have been open to them. They might have chosen to flee from their fear by denying it existed. Their reason might have run something like this. "Let us not admit that there is anything to be alarmed about. We will close our eyes, so to speak, to these roaring waves and imagine that the weather is perfectly calm and sunny. We will stop our ears to this roaring wind, screaming like a wild monster across the waves, and we will imagine that this mad, driving wind is a calm and gentle zephyr blowing in our faces. We will not admit there is anything wrong."

Now, that is the position many of us try to take. We attempt to run from our fears, to act as if they do not exist. In fact, many people try to close their eyes and tiptoe by anything that is unpleasant or frightening. We are like the man Joseph Fort Newton told about who said that he hated to see women standing in buses or subways. He just could not to save his life see women standing while he sat. "What do you do about it?" someone asked him. "Oh," said he, "I close my eyes." There are whole religions that play on our fears and foolishness by telling us just to deny the presence of things that are bad or evil. If you do not admit you're sick, you're not sick, they say. And there is a measure of truth in this, because our minds are powerful allies or enemies. But disease is not often banished by refusing to admit it. Microbes are not usually killed by thoughts but by antibiotics.

Since the day of Jonah, people have been trying to run away from fear, from fact, from truth. No man can run away from fear. He carries himself wherever he goes, and his fear is in him. Life is insecure and sometimes unbearable, but to take a trip will not make it less so, if that is all we do. If there is fear within us, we do not wipe it out by making believe it does not exist. An old familiar hymn says, " 'Tis heaven to be," not in some favorable geographical situation, but " 'Tis heaven to be wherever I be, if Jesus is there."

The disciples might have faced their condition with the decision to fight their fear. They might well have reasoned that since they were in this awful plight they would not panic. They would not allow their fears to get into the saddle. Courage would mark their acts and motivate their spirits. They would do whatever they had to do. They would fight every step of the way, and if they had to go down to a watery grave, they would do it with honor. This is a brave and admirable decision. We still read with admiration of the elder Astor at the sinking of the *Titanic*. He stood at the rail, having put his pregnant wife on board a lifeboat and having calmly waved good-bye to her. He went down to a coffin-less grave in the Atlantic with a calm smile on his face. People will always admire that kind of courage. The heart sort of stands at attention in the presence of gallantry like that. And, surely, the man who has the courage to face whatever it is that terrifies him has taken the first step in conquering it. But courage alone won't make for great adequate living. Bertrand Russell speaks somewhere of a "brave, unyielding despair" in facing the dark defeat which life inevitably entails. Courage is not enough. It is admirable, but it can wear thin and get tired. Just to grit our teeth and clench our jaws and to square our shoulders and take it does not seem to be enough for the sons and daughters of God.

There must be something warmer, more promising than the Arctic splendor of standing with clenched jaw and grim coun-tenance, bravely bearing the slings and arrows of outrageous fortune. What if the glint of some heavenly sunshine can flash on the damp, dark swamps of our terror and our fears? There must be some higher way if God be God. Something finer and fairer than just taking it on the chin. Endurance is not the ulti-mate word of the Christian faith. Victory is the supreme shout of the light centered in Christ.

When Jesus had been awakened by the disciples and had heard their terrors, he calmed the storm. A large part of the fury he tamed may have been the storm in the disciples. Jesus then went into a postmortem analysis, so to speak, of their spiritual plight. He said, "Where is your faith?" Here was his answer to fear. Faith! Not foolish optimism, but faith in the living God. Some-one said, "Fear knocked at the door. Faith opened it and lo, there was no one there. Faith drives fear forth for it rests our case in God's hands." A worthy faith builds on a sure foundation. It rests on the faith that God is in charge of things. No idle luck sits at the heart of the universe, but God is in command of things. No sparrow falls to the ground without God knowing. No child stubs his toe but that the Father knoweth and careth. Underneath are the everlasting arms. We may be called to walk dangerous and treacherous paths, and our road may wind and twist up steep and perilous curves, but we walk not beyond the Father's view. "He knoweth the way that I take." Faith is trusting ourselves in his hands. Faith is leaning on his promises, trusting what he has said, believing that all God has is on the side of love and goodness and righteousness. If I am right, says a part of a hymn, "he'll fight my battle." Faith is a living adventure with God.

Like As a Father

Psalm 103:13

Like as a father pitieth his children, so the LORD pitieth them that fear him. (Psalm 103:13)

The one hundred and third psalm is classic in its stately cadences and in its quiet, strong assertions. It is high religion set to music. I suppose that all of us associate a certain passage of Scripture with a certain event, a time when a hitherto dull, dim passage was flooded with light and meaning by an experience which we can never forget. I associate a part of this psalm with a grateful memory which now reaches over a considerable stretch of time. Years ago our church structure, covering the length of a city block in Brooklyn, was completely destroyed by fire. There came a time when the rebuilding of that structure seemed to be on the edge of failure and despair, for there was no money. On a chill and gloomy November Saturday evening, I walked into the church's temporary quarters, brooding on what looked like the sad end of a bright, bold dream. Among the envelopes of the day's mail was one which bore no return address. Idly and disinterestedly I opened the envelope, and a cashier's check for one thousand dollars, without the giver's signature, fell to the desk. There was only a slip of paper. Almost stunned and trembling, I picked up the sheet of paper, which bore the opening words of the one hundred and third psalm: "Bless the LORD, O my soul: and all that is within me, bless his holy name. Bless the LORD, O my soul, and forget not all his benefits."

That gift was to come annually, until our new structure was cleared of debt. I still do not know the name of the donor, but obviously this grand old psalm had touched that person deeply

---

Sermon delivered October 5, 1969.

and lastingly. And well it might, for this psalm, beginning in such august praise, moves into an explanation of its adoration of God. It runs: "The LORD is merciful and gracious, slow to anger and plenteous in mercy. He hath not dealt with us after our sins: nor rewarded us according to our iniquities. As far as the east is from the west, so far hath he removed our transgressions from us." And then, like a most precious stone among many gems, there are the words "Like as a father pitieth his children, so the LORD pitieth them that fear him."

"Like as a father." This was a tremendous, upward thrust of religious insight when we remember that the idea of God was far removed from this among millions, and still is. "Like as a father, so the LORD. . . . " Well, countless people believe otherwise. God is a leering, lurking enemy waiting to pounce upon unsuspecting folk. Others believe that he is a great shadow darkening the sunniness of life, threatening to swoop down upon us. As such, the deity must be placated, bribed by sacrifices and offerings. The incident of Abraham nearly offering Isaac as a human sacrifice could not have happened if there had not been a day when human sacrifice, even child sacrifice, was an accepted thing. So this view sees God as our enemy, watching, disapproving, anxious to punish us. Then at the height of faith, a little advance copy of the New Testament, this one hundred and third Psalm goes on. "Like as a father pitieth his children, so the LORD pitieth them that fear him." The fathers of the earth ought to take great and justifiable satisfaction in the fact that the highest symbol of God yet known to humanity is that of father.

The word *father* evokes memories for most of us, glad and hallowed, for God in his wisdom has given us mothers and fathers that our emotional balance might be properly established. One of the greatest tragedies which can happen to any people or any family is that of reduction of the status of the father symbol, for God has given fathers in order that we might know the meaning of firmness mixed with tenderness and mothers that we might know tenderness mixed with firmness. When either of these is lacking, emotional imbalance is established and deviations are introduced into a home, a community, a race. Flabby convictions, lack of integrity, and cravenness are often the results of weak father symbols. Like as a father!

Well, we can come to understand a little more of God by looking at earthly fathers, real ones. An earthly father has the need of wisdom. I do not mean by that mere knowledge, but the right use of knowledge, which is wisdom. An earthly father has the need of balancing his desire for the comfort and welfare of his child over and against his need to lead his child into a worthy self-reliance. I sat but recently with a lad whose father tried to substitute things for attention and time. His son's life is a study in failure, and the father's heart is in candidacy for heartbreak.

God is a better father than our earthly fathers, for he knows how to mix gift with effort. He is, as an ancient seer saw, like an eagle who casts the young eaglet forth that in the desperation of falling it might learn to fly. We are born to fly on wings of prayer and faith, but we only learn this when circumstances come pushing us from secure ease to dangerous and dizzying altitudes. As we fall, we instinctively call on our powers to pray and believe and, therefore, to conquer. God mixes enough security with enough risk to make us true sons and daughters of whom he can be proud. He gives us roses but surrounds them with thorns, sunshine but intersperses it with clouds. God gives us springtime, but the chill of winter is his gift also. He gives us the power to laugh but equips us likewise with the capacity to cry. God gives us food from the earth but sets the requirement of sweaty toil that we might eat partly out of our own sacrifice and effort. He gives us births in our families that cradles might gladden the family circle. But the same God gives us the death angel, that the memory of graves might make us see life as a high and swift and solemn transaction. "Sometimes on the mountain where the sun shines so bright, sometimes in the valley in the darkest of night, God leads his dear children along," we sing sometimes in our church.

"Like as a father" means also the power of example. A true father has to reckon what effect what he does will have on his child. A father has told of how he was reduced to tears while walking in a muddy street, only to look back to see his little son straining to make steps that would land him in his father's footsteps. An old friend once told me that he had to stop smoking when his boys were born because he did not want them to smoke. The power of an example is a powerful thing. It enshrines our acts beyond our years and, for good or evil, imparts to us a kind of immortality. "Like as a father." God is our perfect example. We are called upon to be like him. The psalmist cries out somewhere a prayer all heavy with passionate desire, "I shall awake in his likeness." It was Jesus who told us to look to God for our example, not to people. "Be perfect, even as your heavenly Father is perfect."

Sixty years have come and gone since there came to me on the porch of the house where I was reared the sure awareness that no earthly man could ever be a true example, for our idols have feet of clay, and our mighty Achilles always has heels undipped in immunizing, protecting waters. A fellow student, older than I, and now a distinguished educator, was talking about a professor whom he had idolized and who in an hour of testing proved cowardly. Said the student with a heavy lament in his voice, "It is the falling of an ideal." Men will fail, even earthly fathers. You and I do not want to be completely like any man we have ever known, though we have admired some men intensely. Ah, but God is different. There is no quirk or weakness in him. Many who have seen God in the face of Jesus Christ count it worth a lifetime of surrender and seeking, of grand adventure and hazards, if, please God, somewhere on ahead they may see come to pass in their own lives that incredible word which the New Testament utters about what we may yet become. "It does not appear, it says, what we shall be. But this we know, that when he shall appear, we shall be like him, for we shall see him as he is." Arthur Gossip, with that rare gift of disciplined imagining which has belonged to the Scottish preacher, used to say that those who surrender and seek are to become so like Jesus Christ that one day angels, looking first at him and then at those who are his, will not be able to tell him from them.

You will not be letting me off, I hope, with this as the last word. There is a sense, how shall I put it? — in which God is quite clearly not like our fathers. The worthiest among us can scarcely bear to think of our children going into hard suffering, to say nothing of sending them there. We come now upon a mystery in which I so hope you will see some light and guidance and understanding. There is a son, and he is talking earnestly to his father and calls him so. It is Jesus praying in Gethsemane. Listen: "Father, if thou be willing, remove this cup from me. Nevertheless, not my will but thine be done." And he got up and went on to shame and suffering and death, saying with a brave confidence, "The cup which my Father hath given me, shall I not drink it?"

When the tides of life turn against you, do remember that, too, about God. Try to remember that unlike our earthly fathers, he will send us into things that seem too ugly and ominous and painful. But you will remember also, won't you, that unlike our earthly fathers, he knows full well what we can bear and, in bearing, what we can become.

✑ 10 ✑

WHAT ARE YOU DOING HERE?

John 13:34

A new commandment I give unto you, That ye love one another;
as I have loved you, that ye also love one another. (John 13:34)

Someone has told of a bleary-eyed, whisky-logged man wandering into the side door of a downtown church in a Midwestern city and finding himself facing a worshiping congregation. The story runs that this poor, drunken man, somewhat unsteady on his feet, cried out in a loud voice, "Hello, folks, what are you doing here?" The source of the question might be suspect, but the question is quite appropriate. Indeed, about the whole voyage of life the question may be What are you doing here? When the gospel was first preached in England, an old Northumberland nobleman wondered what the new tidings had to say about the mystery of our time on this planet. He reflected that we are like birds which fly in from a dark night, enter the lighted room of life, flutter around a while in the light, and then suddenly fly out through another door into the mysterious darkness of death. What are we doing here?

The Bible speaks in a different tone of our transiency and impermanence in this life. It says that we are "strangers and pilgrims," as all our forebears were, and we have here "no continuing city." First, we are children, and all around us are our elders, apparently so strong, so durable. A few years pass, and we are young men and women. Some of our elders are no longer among us, but we are in the vigor of life and the sun shines brightly on our pathway as we walk with firm and eager stride toward our destiny. A few more seasons pass, and we enter the middle years, still strong, but quiet messages begin to reach us of waning powers and disappearing vitality. Around us there are then so few

Sermon delivered October 12, 1969.

of those who are our elders. We walk well but run poorly. Not many more years slip away before our footsteps are slowed, and our visions are dimmed. Friends have disappeared, and evening is upon us with its fading light and its chill winds.

What does it all mean? People have given many answers to that question. Some have suggested that our point here is to live a long life. Almost all cultures put great store by the length of life. And yet, somehow we reckon that while age is honorable, life is a more serious transaction than mere length, for many of the world's greatest heroes have been those whose lives have been of short duration. I remember my father making great emphasis of the futility of merely living a long time without doing anything. He would quote that biblical passage which says Methuselah lived nine hundred sixty-nine years and died, nothing else, although the Scriptures do say that he fathered offspring. Length of years is not enough. Indeed, it has been said of some public figures that they lived too long to enjoy their brightest luster in history. One thinks of President Woodrow Wilson at the height of his mental powers and political influence, during the days of World War I, only to sink slowly in illness and disillusionment following his gallant but losing effort to bring the United States into the League of Nations.

While long life is greatly to be cherished, this is not why we are here, for the fairest, dearest, lordliest, loveliest life ever lived on this planet came to its earthly end when Jesus died before he was thirty-three years of age. We are surely not here to be forever smiling. Mervin Himbury, the Australian preacher, once said in the Concord pulpit that the old hymn "Now I Am Happy All the Day" does not by any means fully describe the Christian life. There have been those, the hedonists of pagan philosophy, for instance, who have insisted that pleasure is the point of living. When one looks at the toothpaste ads and watches our entertainers, one might be convinced that a smile is the trademark of life. The photographers want us to fake a smile for every picture. "Say cheese," they say, which has absolutely no laughter in the sound of it. We are not here to be merely happy. To have that deep, persuasive, underlying joy of which the New Testament speaks is a legacy open, of course, to each of us. But to be always gaily happy is too shallow a destiny for the sons and daughters of God. We are not a pack of hyenas. A perpetual grin would be an idiot's mask.

There is sorrow and there is sin and there is sickness and there is death in this world, and sometimes we cannot keep on smiling. As a lad in the Louisiana swamp county, I used to hear my elders sing, "Everybody's Got to Cry Sometime." An earlier day in American education, and in the culture's standards, emphasized self-reliance. Do you remember Emerson's essay on self-reliance? When I was a lad, we were drilled in this American virtue. We see this characteristic in the western hero. He is a steely-eyed independent. He needs not the favor of men nor the love of women. He has his horse and his forty-five and he can sit in his saddle for days and sleep on the ground and rustle up his own cooking and brew his own coffee. Self-reliance in its right context is a worthy virtue, but it belongs primarily to a frontier where men rarely brushed shoulders with each other. The continuing popularity of western drama on television may well reflect the yearning in the American mentality for a time when life was simpler, men's obligations to each other spasmodic and infrequent, and each person was on his own.

The truth is that we are not here to be merely self-reliant people. We cannot. At one end of life, the first, we must have others to see about us, for infants cannot see about themselves, while at the other end, when life's sun is setting and old age overtakes us and our footsteps are labored and slow and our hands are palsied and weak, we again need someone to help us on to the end. Too much emphasis on self-reliance is foolishness, for we are meant to be interdependent, not independent. We are members one of another.

Jesus said that we are here that we might fulfill his commandment. One hears him talking to his disciples as the prospect of an early and cruel death becomes an ever more vivid and grim certainty. It is his farewell discourse in the bosom of the fellowship. He is laying to his friends' hearts what he thinks of them and what he expects of them. Then, he puts it to them quite bluntly, places upon them this burden, "This is my commandment, that you love one another even as I have loved you."

This is a planet of pain and a world of disorder. Wherever we look there is confusion. Our country continues a broken and divided land. We are race against race and generation against generation. Our families are under the threat of dissolution, as disintegration of that basic cell of society continues to climb at an incredible rate. And to all this someone says, the best that the Christian gospel can offer is a commandment that we should love one another?

Ah, but this love of which Jesus speaks is not the sugary, sentimental, soft thing of which we think when the word *love* is uttered. Our new-world optimism and Hollywood preoccupation for romantic feelings have taken from this old word its affirmative toughness. On the lips of Jesus, it meant an enlightened, aggressive, relentless will for the good of all people. Even when we accept the meaning of the word as Jesus uttered it, we are likely to believe that our commitment to love one another is private and individual: a cup of cold water to those who thirst, and a piece of bread to those who hunger, one by one as we have opportunity. Praise God, to love one another does involve our personal relations vitally and inescapably, for "the gift without the giver is bare."

At the same time, we have not yet been willing to throw into our great, massive structural arrangements of society the commandment to love one another. To be aggressively committed to the good of all people in our businesses and in our industries seems to most of us utterly too large an order. To be stubbornly determined that our arrangements of government shall be marshaled to the true benefit of all people seems to many of us a little too grandiose for us to conceive. To be led of Jesus means nothing less than throwing in our small strength, all of it, no matter how puny it may seem, with his great strength in the confidence that the tide of battle can be changed by this alliance between him and us. For there is an audacious optimism, realistic and clear-eyed, he offers to those who surrender to him and who make their commitment to love one another.

If Jesus is to be believed, our families and our governments and our industries can be affected vitally and affirmatively by those who have aggressive good will. Again and again on his lips were words of firm and steady assurance about what can happen. Listen to his claim "All things are possible." When a few of his disciples made a modest assault upon the lovelessness of the world, his was a brave shout of confidence about the tide of the battle between all that is right and all that is wrong. Said Jesus, "I saw Satan fall from heaven as lightning." Aggressive good will is a mighty, explosive, expulsive power available to you wherever you are and whatever your circumstance. Indeed, it is the destiny, bright and splendid, to which you are called in every relationship, private and public, in which you find yourself. Really, that's what you and I are meant to be doing here.

INVISIBLE SUPPLIES

John 4:32

But he said unto them, I have meat to eat that ye know not of.
(John 4:32)

Giant fists and midget hearts, university graduates in things physical, kindergarten failures in things spiritual. Thus might we well
describe our day and generation. There have been ages and eras
in which people desired to bless the world but lacked the physical equipment. Ours is an age in which we have the physical
equipment in abundance but lack the spiritual conviction to truly
serve the cause of a world "wherein dwelleth righteousness."
General Douglas MacArthur was never more right than when he
said at the conclusion of the second great war that our world
problem is theological. By this he meant that our great contem-
porary lacks are interior and spiritual, expressing themselves in
deranged outward manifestations of personal conduct and public
irresponsibility.

You and I have countless visible supplies but lack those invisible supplies without which life is lame and inadequate. One has
only to look around at our material achievements to realize what
a sleek and competent generation we are on the outside. Ours is
a chrome-plated, stainless steel, swift age. Our modern communications are instantaneous, not only from one area of the earth
to another but also from planet to planet as we discovered in the
gallant odyssey of our young and old astronauts to the moon.
Being able to talk from planet to planet, we seem to have so
little worth saying on either an intraplanetary or an interplane-
tary basis. About our communications from planet to planet, one
cannot help wondering at the same time if we plan to insult the

Sermon delivered October 19, 1969.

far reaches of space with the flippant, sometimes obscene, shallow chatter to which we are so often treated in our various forms of communication.

Our ability to make ourselves understood to one another can be illustrated in our long and shameful failure to establish a healing and purposeful dialogue in America's perennial problem of race. Blacks and whites use the same words but give to them vastly different meanings. To one, law means affirmatively upholding the constitution as to the rights of all Americans. To the other, law means swiftly punishing those who step outside of it. Both are valid aspects of the word, but we Americans seem unable to give to this word *law* its true and full meaning.

Our visible resources are in great supply. Alas, those qualities of soul by which we communicate with wholeness and integrity are so woefully in short supply. When I was younger, men spoke with bated breath of the possibility of a person having one meal in New York and the next in Los Angeles. We are now being told that presently it will be commonplace for people to travel from New York to Los Angeles between meals, though it may still take from dinner to breakfast to get from the airport into the city. Having such enormous visible supplies in the matter of movement, and I am told that we Americans are the most mobile nation in history, we are the same restless, discontented, uneasy people when we arrive at our destination as we were when we boarded the plane for departure. Indeed, our determination to be on the move may itself be a symptom of our inability to make peace within ourselves, our impoverishment of invisible spiritual supplies.

In the much closer geographical context of family life, our physical comforts are beyond the wildest imaginings of earlier generations. Think of the comforts and conveniences in your own family: washing machines, swift automobiles, air conditioners, hair dryers and on and on, and yes, for the young, the ever-present, full-volume listening devices. Many of these save a great deal of time, but do they give us more time for each other? In so many families we lack the inner grace to listen to each other, to say nothing of being able to enter upon those times of silence in which a deep and unutterable communion of spirit with spirit occurs.

The good news of the gospel is that we can have deep, invisible interior supplies of the spirit which strengthen and sustain us in all the shifting circumstances of these lives of ours. There is a scene in the life of Jesus which strikingly sets this forth. Jesus was waiting for the return of his disciples when he happened to meet a Samaritan woman, which meeting ended in one of the most touching conversations and consequences in the Gospels. While waiting, he met the woman of Samaria. They talked. Later his disciples returned. By that time a crowd had come from the woman's village to hear this man about whom she had said, "Come see a man that told me everything about myself." His disciples, having brought food, were anxious for him to eat. He, however, said to the disciples, "I have meat to eat you do not know about."

Now, this was no comment of scorn about physical needs. There were early heresies within the church which tried to minimize our Lord's humanity in order to exalt his divinity. They sought to say that the Son of God could not suffer, could not thirst, could not get hungry. Indeed, my late and dear seminary roommate, Dr. James Cayce, said that this heresy claimed that Christ was off on the Mount of Olives laughing at the crucifixion. As God, he could not suffer. But here is the mystery of the Incarnation. Jesus Christ, very man, very God, did get hungry and thirsted and said so, became sad and cried. He said, in the midst of that most familiar prayer which he taught, the words pure and simple, "Give us this day our daily bread."

Christians cannot abandon this world and its needs. We must work for physical changes. This is the ancient tension of the people of God. This is a dying world, and yet God's people must speak to it the word of life. You and I must not flee or sidestep the responsibility of trying to make this world a little more like God would have it. Jesus did not say to his people to flee from the earth's affairs but said rather, "Go ye into all the world." He would have changed to his will all of the world, business, politics, pleasure, every area of life.

Suppose people will not hear? Suppose our best efforts fail? Suppose the wicked flourish and the righteous suffer? If the visible results are disappointing and paltry, we need invisible supplies, resources of the Spirit. This is overcoming religion, because it is based not on what circumstances are but upon what God is in our lives, what he is now and what we believe he will be in the future. "I have meat to eat ye know not of." There are available resources of the Spirit that strengthen and sustain us in the hardest hours so that we discover we have strength we did not dream we possessed. The world cannot give this, but God can give it. This now of which I speak is the legacy of those who believe worthily. It is the kind of spiritual calm which you and I need and which is above strife and stress. This kind of spiritual supply is affected but not determined by outward circumstances.

I notice that invisible spiritual wealth in some of the songs of the American slaves, which continue to haunt the imagination and conscience of the country and indeed of the world. In an incredibly pinched and grim circumstance, there leapt out of deep interior spiritual resources, the beauty of, "I'm so glad, trouble don't last always," and from a poverty so deep that they could not even call their bodies their own, they dared to see bright, splendid possessions and sang, "Looked all around me, it looked so fine, asked my Lord if it all was mine." Well, I'll not ask you to ignore what is around you, your own set of conditions. It would be criminal for me to do that. But surely you can see that you need not be determined by your circumstances. I remember as a boy hearing my father preaching and using an example from Charles Lindbergh's then almost unbelievable flight over the Atlantic. He said Mr. Lindbergh reported that he came upon a fierce Atlantic storm. It was impossible to navigate through it. The clouds were dark and heavy. The dauntless young pilot turned the fragile *Spirit of St. Louis* to the right and then to the left, but in both directions the storm raged. Lindbergh chose to climb upward, and there he found that strange and cloudless calm at which air travelers often marvel. This is possible in your daily living. You can move in the midst of disaster and of difficulty and yet, in another sense, live above it. Thank God that there is an interior wealth of spiritual power and authority which is your birthright and by which you can determine your circumstance.

So many of us would discover, were we to appropriate this, that things which have left us defeated and wilted would fall into their proper place, and we would discover a sense of power and a sense of adequacy of which we did not dream ourselves capable. This is not something open to any secret few. This is a capacity and a power available to any person who will have it. It is a part of our spiritual birthright as the sons and daughters of God. There is a power which is available to us which we can have if we will. And if our circumstances cannot be altered, what is more important is that this internal exuberance can give you joy and peace in the midst of hard trials and heavy loads? This is available to you. Appropriate it now. It is yours!

✎ 12 ✎

THE MYSTERY OF SPIRITUALITY

John 3:8

The wind bloweth where it listeth, and thou hearest the sound thereof, but canst not tell whence it cometh, and whither it goeth: so is every one that is born of the Spirit. (John 3:8)

"The wind bloweth where it will, and thou hearest the sound thereof, but cannot tell whence it cometh and whither it goeth. So is everyone that is born of the Spirit." These words were spoken during a conversation which two men had in the stillness of a Jerusalem evening. One of the men was Jesus, carpenter of Nazareth, become prophet from Galilee. The other man who talked in the Palestinian darkness that night was Nicodemus, member of the Sanhedrin, become seeker after everlasting truth. The word floated through to Nicodemus that Jesus of Nazareth was talking about a new birth. Now, Nicodemus was not one to rest his case upon some uncertain gossip. He was not willing to reach a conclusion on a rumor. He was a man of the law and a believer in firsthand testimony. He decided to go and talk to Jesus himself. He would not send a messenger, for the report might be distorted or garbled. He would seek himself to find out just what the situation was.

There is really no other way to find a sustaining faith except in personal venture. Donald Hankey, once so widely known in this country and so beloved in his native England, used to say in his striking way that being a Christian means betting one's life on God. The Bible is replete with almost unbelievably rich promises, but almost all of them are built upon some condition which we must fulfill. "Come unto me, all ye that labor and are heavy laden, and I will give you rest." This is true biblical humanism,

---

Sermon delivered October 26, 1969.

with its recognition of vast capacities that are in us. This is refutation of the tired old claim that the faith of Christ is for weaklings and cowards and the passively inactive. Far from it! There is a call to action which rings like a trumpet on almost every page of the New Testament. Nicodemus decided to confront the man from Nazareth with the deepest concernments of his life. Likewise, we shall find strength and empowerment in him only as we make our move in his direction. No amount of armchair speculation will clear for us our doubts.

On the other hand, Jesus Christ does not depend on any dim light or vagueness in order to pass muster in people's esteem and faith. He does not rely upon any fast sleight of hand in order to hold followers. He invites investigation, opens himself to any who will examine, as he did to those sharpest little detectives of insincerity when he said, "Suffer the little children to come unto me, and forbid them not." I like the word of the angel at the Resurrection. There was no attempt to hustle away those who came or to divert their attention as if some piece of quick-handed magic was about to be done which could not bear scrutiny. The word of the angel was, rather, "Come, see the place where the Lord lay." Mark this, the only way you are going to have a strong, vibrant faith is by confronting the claims of Christ with trustfulness and obedience.

The winds of gossip which bore to Nicodemus rumors of a teacher talking about a new birth, a fresh start, with the slate wiped clean, intrigued and haunted the doctor of laws. What a wild, preposterous notion! But what if, by whatever stretch of the imagination, it could actually happen? Suppose a man could really get a new start in life? And so in the evening shadows, this man of the law talked with the Son of Man. There was no question about whether there need be a new start, only how could it be possible.

In you as in me, there is surely the same longing which Nicodemus brought to Jesus in the Jerusalem night. All of us sense a profound disquiet at the heart of life, a painful awareness that we have made far less of this gift of existence than we might have. This is the age-old question. I think that wherever people

have thought seriously about the nature and destiny of life, they
have recognized that we human beings are not what we ought
to be. The quality of "oughtness" belongs alone to the sons and
daughters of earth. The instinct of the possible, as over against
the actual, is the peculiar legacy of humankind. The pleasure and
pain of us all are that we long to be better and other than what
we are. Whatever our plight, whatever the time, there is that
yearning. The old hymn has it

> Though like the wanderer,
> The sun gone down,
> Darkness be over me,
> My rest a stone,
> Yet in my dreams I'd be
> Nearer, my God, to thee.

Yes, but if this insanely wonderful possibility can belong to us,
then how bring it off? How can we drop these heavy habits of
flesh, so promising in prospect, so empty in retrospect? How can
a freshness descend upon these tired and worn spirits of ours?
How can we know again the crisp freshness of the morning?

So a man long ago, spokesman, really, for each one of us,
raised the mystery of man's helplessness in the face of his aspirations. How? If Nicodemus raised the mystery of human inability,
Jesus in turn raised the mystery of spirituality, of a presence unseen and yet decisive, and all around us. He said to Nicodemus,
"The wind bloweth where it will." What is the wind? Air in motion, someone say. What is air? Gases, nitrogen and oxygen and
other chemicals. But no one seems to know quite where the air
originates and why it is here, and yet nobody can doubt its presence. The meteorological experts detect the wind and sometimes
accurately forecast its movements, but they cannot order its direction or intensity. The wind is unseen, but it is felt, and its presence
cannot be doubted. What Jesus was saying to Nicodemus and to
us is that there is a presence in history and around each of us,
unseen by the natural eye and yet surpassingly real, the presence
of God. Have you not felt in joy or sorrow the mood of the man
who mused long ago, "Whither shall I go from thy spirit, and
whither shall I flee from thy presence? If I ascend up into heaven,

thou art there. If I make my bed in hell, behold, thou art there. If I take the wings of the morning and dwell in the uttermost parts of the sea, even there shall thy hand lead me, and thy right hand shall hold me." There is a presence, sustaining what is decent and good, frustrating what is wrong and evil.

With that presence, we must come to terms in history and in ourselves. In our country, we have been haunted by one great, unresolved issue. It is so well known that it is hardly necessary to mention what it is. Our peculiar problem of race casts a shadow over the founding fathers. Thomas Jefferson, speaking of slavery, said that he feared for the nation when he remembered that God is just. This evil of racism in America's souls brought us to our great national heartbreak in the battlefields of our civil conflict, names that now haunt the national memory and echo with an infinite sadness: Antietam, Gettysburg, Vicksburg, Port Hudson, Appomattox. Who can doubt that a presence has been among us, frustrating all our attempts, to resolve what is wrong until we resolve it right? A hundred years and more have come and gone, and still there hangs over us this specter, threatening, dividing, confusing, crippling, compromising our true national greatness.

There is a God in history, like the wind unseen, but, like the wind, powerful, pervasive, sometimes gentle like a zephyr, sometimes angry like a hurricane. Too many people have witnessed to a sense of presence for any of us to dismiss the idea lightly. One hears Isaiah's word of witness, "The spirit of the Lord is upon me," or Ezekiel saying, "So the spirit of the Lord lifted me up and took me away, and I went in bitterness, in the heat of my spirit; but the hand of the Lord was strong upon me." Who can forget Jesus echoing Isaiah's word across many centuries and taking a vow of purpose in those words that still thrill the heart, "The spirit of the Lord is upon me, because he hath anointed me to preach the gospel to the poor; he hath sent me to heal the brokenhearted, to preach deliverance to the captives, and recovering of sight to the blind, to set at liberty them that are bruised, to preach the acceptable year of the Lord."

George Frederick Handel's name has become a household word throughout Christendom because of his *Messiah*. Thousands of tourists annually look for his place in the poet's corner at West-minster Abbey. When his great oratorio was presented, and as the mighty swell of the triumphant climax of the chorus was heard, King George II stood in recognition of a mightier monarch, the King of kings, wherewith the whole assemblage stood, inaugurat-ing a custom which we still follow. Handel's great work, if we are to believe him, did not flow alone out of the musical genius of the composer. He said, "I did think I did see all heaven before me, and the great God upon his throne." All around you now is that presence, unseen and yet real, like the wind. It is actually true that in Jesus Christ you can come into a new birth where that old and worn spirit of yours is made fresh like the morning and radiant like sunrise. Like the wind, the presence is there, and all of the old enslavements can be dismissed and passed, and what is bro-ken in you can be made whole. And in the power of Jesus Christ you can walk forth into what one of his people once called "the glorious liberty of the sons of God."

∽ 13 ∾

A TOTAL ANSWER

Proverbs 3:6

In all thy ways acknowledge him, and he shall direct thy paths.
(Proverbs 3:6)

God knows, we need some answers that will stand up in our lives. Someone has said that history consists mainly of the same mistakes being made over and over again. So Oswald Spengler in his *Decline of the West* would echo. Maybe so or maybe not. But our personal history surely consists so much of fancy answers to life's issues that fail us over and over again. Every time we think we have found the key to the strange mystery of living, a new situation enters the field of experience and baffles our supposed solution. I thought I knew the answer, we think. But something has gone awry and left our souls bewildered and puzzled. Now and then we grow hard and cynical about everything and everybody because we have been betrayed or misled. We decide that never again will we put our trust in anything or anybody. Just when we wallow in the deepest trough of skepticism, some unexpected kindness is done to us or some totally unmerited favor is shown to us, putting all our doubt under assault, and we begin to feel that our skepticism and distrust are all too brittle and cheap. As Browning has it in such shining words, "Just when we are safest, there's a sunset touch, a fancy from a flower bell, someone's death, a chorus ending from Euripedes." And all of a sudden, the gray skies are sunlit again and the rain-misted hills glisten once more.

We may think life's answer is pleasure, but in our soberest moments we know that while pleasure may be the sauce of life, it can never be the meat. We may think the answer is success, but it

---

Sermon delivered November 2, 1969.

so quickly turns to ashes or, still fresh, becomes so empty when our souls cry out for other sustenance. We may think the answer is money, until we read of someone who has more than his share of it committing suicide or making such a mess of his life that we are driven to pity him, though heaven knows we have far less of this world's goods than he.

The Bible has only one answer for all life's ills. It is stated succinctly and powerfully in one of the wisdom books of Israel, the book of Proverbs. Here is contained the tested and distilled wisdom of a people's long and checkered history. The only ultimate, unassailable answer to life is God, it says. "In all thy ways acknowledge him, and he shall direct thy paths." That's the Bible's answer. It is not the answer of a creed, for no creed can do more than mirror reality and echo the authentic experience of truth. The Bible's answer to all of life is God, not philosophy, since no philosophy can contain the welter and variety of human experience. "In all thy ways, acknowledge God, and he shall direct thy path."

How hard a lesson! How long we have been in learning it. What sorrow we have endured while learning. What heartbreak we have known because we have not heeded that message. We flounder and stumble and puzzle and go down to dark despair and clouded hopelessness, when there it stands like a mighty beacon on a stormy, starless sea: In all thy ways acknowledge God, and he shall direct thy path. In all thy ways, that would include relating our hopes and dreams to God. It is the province of young people to hold for themselves great hopes and splendid visions of what they might become. This is their heritage and their birthright. Older people commit a crime if they try to reduce the aspirations of young people. This is the sacrament of youth, and you who are young have a right to dream vast dreams and scan the distant horizons. Again, this is your birthright. Nevertheless, the time of youth's bright hopes can be a desperate, painful period. A friend once said to me that there was a time in his youth when he was subject to moods of deep depression and great fear. The reason, he said, was that he was so afflicted with doubt as to whether he could bring off what he wanted to do and become the kind of man he wanted to be. Yes, youth is a time of high, vast dreams. But doubts afflict also, and there are so many pitfalls. All of us looking back on our youth wonder, as Mahalia Jackson sings, "how we got over."

Nothing is more tragic about the long season of injustice in this country than what it has done to so many young people and to their hopes and aspirations. At the same time, no disadvantaged young person ought to let the delinquencies of society make a delinquent of him. I know the problems such young people face, but I know the answer also: "In all thy ways acknowledge him, and he shall direct thy path." Nothing is more sad or wistful than the plight of those who pass the morning years and realize that most of the bright possibilities they once cherished and followed will never come true.

All of us have to come to accept ourselves and to admit that our reach has exceeded our grasp. For so many of us are so far short of where we meant to be. We had dreams of progress and saintliness that are but bruised memories now. We know within ourselves that we will never be what we once thought was our sure destiny. Time is running out now, and so little of our job is done. The sun is going down on so many of our heads, and we are a long way from home. More than one of us sees himself or herself mirrored in a ragged wreck of a man, met by Bishop Hazen Werner in the East India dock section in London. The man, all unkempt and ragged and dirty, shuffled out of the shadows to beg Bishop Werner for the price of a meal, and said, "I know I've no right to stop you, and if the bobbies stop me, it will be off to Brixham Prison for me. Please sir, pardon me for stopping you all dirty like I am, but you've no notion, sir, the man I meant to be."

How true in varying degrees is this of all of us. We meant to be more than we have become, and now it's almost all over. In our faults, acknowledge him and ask for forgiveness, and he will direct our paths. In our failures, acknowledge him. Always there are those who are wrestling with giant enemies who overpower them and strike them down and trample upon them. Sickness fastens its iron grip upon someone we love, and we are powerless to do anything about it. It is all so frustrating and defeating. Or there is that old habit, that despised thing you fought so long. Once it seemed you were on the way to winning the fight, but back it came with a fury and a terrible might to wrestle you to the ground and to chain you again. Today it seems there isn't much use in trying any longer. The one reliably steadying resource you have in your struggle is that God is there, standing with you in the good fight, sustaining, rallying you.

The recognition of an abiding presence and power in our lives does for us a most necessary thing. The sense of God helps us not to think more highly of ourselves than we ought to, for in awareness of him as source of life we become sensitive to our creatureliness, to the fact that we are neither source nor center of life. The temptation to identify ourselves as the most important entity in the world is cause for so much of the suffering and heartbreak in the community of humanity. This weird disease of self-centeredness creates the foundation for racism, turns our family relationships into tense struggles for attention and priority, prostitutes friendship into a tool for the satisfaction of our own warped egos. The tendency to think more highly of ourselves than we ought robs us of the unutterable joy of thankfulness, since our gratitude for the bounties of life is diminished by our belief that we merit whatever good things have happened to us.

Likewise, the failure to acknowledge God in terms of our blessings denies to us a direction toward which we may look with thankful hearts and psalms of praise. You will have heard of a well-known unbeliever saying impulsively on a gloriously beautiful day, "I am so thankful for this day." "To whom, my dear?" asked the friend. So you and I, looking about at all the good which has attended our way, need some direction in which we can turn to express the gratefulness of our hearts that the ways and walks of our lives are as well with us as they are. To have the joy of family, a friend, or daily work is a rich and marvelous blessing. To have someone, God, to whom we can turn to give thanks multiplies with glad thanksgiving the day of the blessing. So we are doubly blessed when we look to God in thanksgiving, blessed once by the blessing and blessed the second time by the joy of thanksgiving. "In all thy ways acknowledge him, and he will direct thy path." This is the legacy of your sonship and daughterhood to God. Never forsake it. Never forget it. Claim it. Seize it. It belongs to you. "In all thy ways acknowledge him, and he will direct thy path."

∽ 14 ∽

A GOSPEL FOR THOSE WHO ARE AFRAID

John 6:20

But he saith unto them, It is I; be not afraid. (John 6:20)

The gospel is good news. The whole gospel is good news for all of our desperate questions, for all of our poignant needs, for all of our mute pleas, for all of our fitful moods and gloomy emotions. The gospel is also good news for all of our anxieties and fears. There is an arresting scene about fear in the New Testament. A little boat was bearing the disciple band from one side of the Sea of Galilee to the other. The sky-blue surface of this calm and placid lake is six hundred feet below sea level, and sudden winds whipping from the valleys of the surrounding mountains can fan these peaceful waters into wild and frothing waves in a matter of seconds. There came a storm at sea. Light banter suddenly turned into frantic cries. Eyes which but a moment before had been lighted with laughter were now glassy with terror. Muscles which but a second ago were relaxed and easy were now taut and strained. The disciples were afraid. Stark consternation raced through their ranks. The fear of a watery grave drove all reason from their minds and froze their hearts with a terrible dread. Jesus, worn from the labors of the day, calm in his confidence in the Father above, lay asleep.

Suddenly the disciples realized that they were helpless and terrified. They ran to where their friend lay asleep in the wildly tossed boat. Their fear-palsied hands were laid rudely on him to arouse him from slumber. On their lips was a fearful plea, a wildly blurted exhortation, a desperate request for aid, "Lord, save us, we perish." Suddenly awakened, distressed by their needless fears, startled by their groundless dread, as if forgetting that God was still sitting King of the floods, he said to them, "Why

Sermon delivered November 9, 1969.

76

are you so fearful, o ye of little faith?" Then he spoke, and the storm passed. Leslie Weatherhead says that Jesus spoke as much to the storm in their hearts as he did to the storm on the sea, bidding their terrors to be calm, putting at peace their wild, distressed fears, the point of the narrative being that Christ is more than a match for our fears.

Surely our generation needs a gospel which can speak to our fears. We are afraid. Of course, fear is a precious native endowment. It is our alarm clock in the moment of peril. A person without fear is a fool and worse. There is a parable in the Gospel of Luke of a judge who feared not God nor regarded man. Is it any wonder he is called an unjust judge? He might also be called an insane one. Fear has blessed our world. People, afraid of ignorance, have built schools. People, afraid of sickness, have erected hospitals. And people, afraid of lawlessness and disorder, have formed governments. People, afraid of tyranny and slavery, have refused to obey unjust laws at the cost of their own lives. This healthy instinct, however, can drive us nearly mad when it is in the saddle, making us neurotic, unreasoning, and turning life into a nightmare.

So many of us are afraid of so many things. There was a time when we spoke of death as our greatest fear, but life, having grown complex and baffling, many more of us are afraid of life. We are afraid of our friends, since the hectic pace of modern city life gives us so little time to make friendship real and deep. We are afraid for our children, since they must live in a nervous, jittery age when the evil of war and the danger of narcotics may prey on their bodies and minds. We are afraid for ourselves since there lurks in each of us a deep marsh of evil and sin, of treachery and betrayal. Many are even afraid of whatever religion they have, since it drives them with demands they cannot meet and places upon them yokes they cannot bear. Alfred Houseman speaks the creed of so many godless, helpless, driven, fearful people of our age of rush and ruin, of anxiety and aspiring, when he cries out, "And how am I to face the odds of man's bedevilment and God's? I, a stranger and afraid, in a world I never made?" Who can exhaust the list? We are afraid of sickness, sorrow, suffering, of jobs that seem too much for us, of the crowd that waits to snare, of husbands and of wives whose love we do not quite trust. A lot of our boldest, loudest talk is done to cover the fears we feel and which frustrate us and make us ashamed.

The gospel is for those who are afraid. First, it gives us the status of possessed people. Second, the gospel gives us a place where we can air our fears and place our pleas. And then, the gospel gives us a partner, a companion to go with us through whatever we are called to pass. One of the reasons for our fears is that we appear to be loose in the world, unowned and therefore not listed on anybody's sheet of assets. To be but dust with the mockery of dreams in it is a terrible fate. To have no relationship to anybody big enough to protect us is perhaps reason for terror. I suppose one of the reasons so many modern people are stricken with fear is because they have no sense of being possessed and owned by God. They feel themselves adrift, spiritually displaced persons, wandering aimlessly across the face of their years.

What a difference it is to be worthily owned. There was a day in Jewish history when the nation was under peril of invasion from the Moabites and Ammonites. The whole populace gathered before the tabernacle and called on God for deliverance. The Scriptures say that all the men of Judea stood before the Lord with their wives and their children. They looked to God as a possessed people would look to their master and protector. The answer was "be not afraid nor dismayed by reason of their great multitude, for the battle is not yours but the Lord's." Jesus tells us over and over, the very hairs of your head are all numbered. Fear you not therefore. We need to be owned. Our flight to false freedom is a flight to fear, for we were born to be worthily possessed. Parents own us and protect us while we are children. When we are grown and the fitful fever of life is upon us, we need a heavenly Father to possess and to keep us. Thus possessed, we have a hiding place, the shadow of a great rock and refuge, as the Bible says.

The good news of the New Testament is that we have also a place to pour out our fears and to make our petitions known. The psychologists tell us that one of the dangers of our fears is that they get repressed, driven down and back into our inmost selves where they spread their venom and secrete their poison. Thus kept within, fear turns the meadows of our souls into dismal swamps, growing their awful plants of dread and terror. What a privilege to be able to lay our fears and anxieties before God. This is the gospel. These men on the stormy sea remembered that they had someone in the boat with them to whom they could cry, "Lord, save us, we perish." Each of us has available an appointed place where we can sob out our deepest fears, lance their festering sores, and open them to the sunlight of healing. There is a secret place of prayer where the soul can bow and cry unashamed and tell God things we dare not utter to any person. There is a trysting place where God does wait to hear and bless his people's deepest needs. How many souls have forded their rivers and have risen from their valleys because they found in God a place to report their anxieties and troubles?

This gospel to the afraid gives us a sense of a partner who goes it with us. The sense of loneliness and abandonment in modern life is almost unbearable. We move in crowds but are lonely. No friend can sit with us in the shadowed recesses of our inmost dreads. There is sickness in life and there is great sorrow, and there is at last the bleak fact of death, and before it a thousand gnawing fears. The disciples remembered Jesus was on board. They were there. The storm was there. Fear was there. But Jesus was there, also. That made the difference. We have a partner. In the distant years of my childhood, we had a saying in the Creole bayou country, with its eerie willow trees and mysterious swamps. If night fell while we were still at play and there was a dark part of the way home, low-hanging trees where fright would freeze young hearts, we had a term. We would ask our friends, "Would you go a *piece of the way* home with me?" Through that lonely stretch of the road! There is that big, strange, silent house that we all fear between me and the light of home. Will you go "a piece of the way"?

The gospel tells of a friend who does not go "a piece of the way" but to the end of the last mile of our mortal journey. Now, here is the difference which high religion makes. It does not promise us exemption from those experiences of joy and sorrow, pain and pleasure which belong to all people. Any religion which does so promise is a shabby possession soon to be revealed as counterfeit and deceiving. A worthy religion looks unblinkingly and honestly at all those ills to which we are heir, and having recognized them for what they are, celebrates the glorious confidence that we are conquerors, and in that daring word of the New Testament, "more than conquerors" in the midst of whatever it is that would otherwise terrify us and crush us. No exemption, but strength, more than enough. Listen to this word: "O Israel, Fear not, for I have redeemed thee, I have called thee by thy name; thou art mine. When thou passest through the waters, I will be with thee; and through the rivers, they shall not overflow thee; when thou walkest through the fire, thou shalt not be burned; neither shall the flame kindle upon thee. For I am the LORD thy God."

∽ 15 ∽

EDEN BEYOND INNOCENCE

Genesis 3:1–24

And the LORD God planted a garden eastward in Eden; and there he put the man whom he had formed. (Genesis 2:8)

There lingers on the edge of human memory a mood, a notion, a half thought, a vague awareness that once somewhere things were far better than they are now. It is the notion of paradise lost, so deeply textured in the reflections of people of almost all origins. The profoundly moving account of Eden tells the story of a glorious, innocent state in which humans once dwelt in this earth and how that happy condition was lost to them because of their transgression and violation of the holy law of God. We have here in this ancient narrative a vivid and moving explanation of what life is all about, with its lost rapture as a result of rupture and separation from God. Eden, as the ancient Israelites recorded, was an ineffably beautiful place. Lush foliage leapt out of the fertile soil everywhere. Flowers of dazzling beauty blossomed wherever the eye could turn. Cool, sparkling water gushed from subterranean fountains here and there. Luscious fruit hung heavy on countless trees. Brooks sang soft songs which charmed the mind and stilled the soul. Eden was an ineffably beautiful place. The richness of the soil produced grain and vegetables of perfect taste and nutrition. The sun beamed ever so gaily and bright, like perpetual springtime. Eden must have been an ineffably beautiful place.

Through its gracious domain walked the assigned ruler of all this splendor and beauty, Adam, man, and at his side, Eve, woman. You wives might want to remind your husbands and you husbands might want to remind your wives of a lovely old word

---

Sermon delivered November 16, 1969.

81

from Andrew Maclaren, which said that woman was not created out of man's head to surpass him, nor from his feet to be trampled upon, but from his side to be his equal, and near his heart to be dear to him. At any rate, as the ancient account runs, as man walked the garden no discord jarred the calmness of his spirit. He was innocent and at peace. Tears were strangers, and sighs were unknown. The grim hand of death had never reached forth to touch and wither human life, and sorrow was an unknown alien in this garden. Man was at peace in his innocence. No sense of shame was upon him. There were no plots in his mind and no anger in his heart. It was the age of beauty and innocence.

Does this ancient account explain our plight? If somehow and somewhere the children of men did not know a world in which peace and beauty were supreme, how then can we explain the notion, so deeply embedded in us, that beauty is right and natural? Why do we not take, rather, to ugliness, unless beauty somewhere and somehow was our natural environment? And how else shall we explain the craving for peace in our hearts if war and carnage are the only legacy we have? Ah, no, this old account speaks a deep and persuasive truth.

Something happened in Eden. There was a break, says the old account, between God and humanity. With all of the areas over which the tenants were given control and dominion, there was one forbidden area, one "thou shalt not," one off limits. Life moves by opposites. Any "thou shalt" implies a "thou shalt not." For every up there is a down. For every right there is a wrong. Strangely enough, it was that prohibition to which Adam and Eve were drawn. The temptation came in an appeal to a doubt, to uncertainty about the honesty of God and the reliability of the given law. In this simple but searching account, the serpent, the personification of evil, is not at the outset ugly and repulsive. There is a subtle grace and an initial attractiveness about the deadly enemy. There is no out-and-out challenge of the law and justice of God. "Hath God said you shall not eat of every tree in the garden?" The question being raised, the first sinister and subtle doubt being aroused, the tempter goes on to say boldly that such is not the case at all. You shall not surely die. God knows that in the day you eat of that tree your eyes shall be opened and you shall be as gods, knowing good and evil.

And so the transgression, the overstretching, the passing of the bounds of limitation, the attempt to be what we are not. Is this the fatal weakness in our humanity? Endowed with so much, we would have more. Made a little lower than God, we would be equal. The age-old lie betrays as it has betrayed ever since. The early beauty passes, and innocence is lost. God appears in the garden, for there is never the power to escape him. There is nowhere to secret oneself from those eyes that follow. Listen to Francis Thompson:

> I fled Him, down the nights and down the days;
> I fled Him, down the arches of the years;
> I fled Him, down the labyrinthine ways
> of my own mind; and in the midst of tears
> I hid from Him, and under running laughter.
>
> Up vistaed hopes I sped:
> and shot precipitated adown titanic glooms of chasmed fears,
> from those strong feet that followed, followed after.
>
> But with unhurrying chase,
> and unperturbed pace,
> Deliberate speed, majestic instancy,
> They beat — and a Voice beat
> more instant than the Feet —
> "All things betray thee, who betrayest Me."

So a guilty man and an offended God enact the drama of divine justice and human sin. "Adam, where art thou?" "I was afraid because I was naked," comes back the answer.

The end of it all is a closed paradise. There is a fateful and ominous sound, a note of doom and the echo of a terrible sorrow. So he drove out the man and woman. The innocence of Adam and Eve had passed. An angel with a flaming sword prevented the expelled sinners from ever returning. They must go through brambles and briars to some future unknown to them, but they cannot go back.

There are many people in this great country of ours who long for America to return to a simpler way, to roll the clock back.

This country is no longer primarily a nation of the countryside where everyone knows everyone, dresses alike, to some extent looks alike, and more or less thinks alike. In this country, the old, simple prejudices and preferences will never again work, nor will force of arms bring that day again, for a people who come to rely solely on force become the slaves of that force and might. God has willed a nobler role for this land, has blessed it beyond belief and ordained that it shall bear his bright dream of a family of humankind united to the ends of the earth. Woe to us if we fail him. The longing to get back to some simple Eden is strong, but this is vain. The past is a closed garden. A flaming sword swings to and fro before its gates. We cannot go back. There is only one way now, and it is on into the future with whatever uncertainty there is.

I would point out that Eden is not the last garden in the Bible; it is the first. There are other gardens. Gethsemane is there, suggesting some solemn acceptance of a high and costly road. And on at the end, in the last book of the Bible, there is another garden, a new Eden. Between the two gardens there is a long and arduous way, and the bright presence of Jesus Christ. The last Eden is not built upon a simple and childish innocence, but knowing all there is to know of the world's ugliness and men's meanness, there comes a new grace and there comes a new power, a new calm, a new adequacy. Listen: "And he showed me a pure river of water of life, clear as crystal, proceeding out of the throne of God and of the lamb. In the midst of the street of it, and on either side of the river, was there the tree of life, which bare twelve manner of fruits and yielded her fruit every month, and the leaves of the tree were for the healing of the nations." That is beyond innocence! We can never go back now. We can never go back to the place where we believe that all people are kind and just. That is the mood of the first Eden. We know better. We can never go back to the simple, innocent Eden when we believed in this country that if only what was wrong was brought to the attention of the nation there was enough good will, enough justice, enough decency to set it right quickly, and in our day and generation it would all come out right. That innocence is gone now. We know now that partisan passion, sectional preferences, and racist prejudices are strong in this land.

We cannot get back to that early innocence, but there is another Eden toward which we can now move. It is founded not upon innocence, but upon faith that there is a power which makes for righteousness. The new Eden is seen by those who have faith that the power of God makes stronger the armies of right than the armies of wrong can ever hope to be, and though often detained by our opposition, God's truth goes marching on. You and I, most of us, cannot get back ever to the Eden of our innocent childhood. We have gone too far. But by the power of Christ we can come to a new Eden beyond the first one of innocent purity. We can never return to the unwrinkled beauty of childhood trust, but the beauty of the Lord can be upon us. We cannot stand in the Eden of childhood hopes, but we can live in the new Eden of faith in God. We cannot return to the Eden of other years, when we had so much confidence in ourselves. We can go on to that Eden where we believe that the Lord will make us sufficient unto whatever we must face and do.

Of course, this Eden on ahead is real and abiding. It is founded upon mature wisdom and not superficial notion. This is the difference between the first Eden and the last one. The last one is not subject to whim or mood. A man of faith, reflecting upon it in another time, once said, "All things work together for good to them that love the Lord," meaning that there is a royal purpose in history and in your history. So don't look back. Look ahead! On ahead the sun is shining. On ahead the flowers are blooming. On ahead the gates of another Eden swing wide.

⌒ 16 ⌒

A Question Out of the Darkness

Luke 7:18–22

And the disciples of John shewed him of all these things. And John calling unto him two of his disciples sent them to Jesus, saying, Art thou he that should come? or look we for another? When the men were come unto him, they said, John [the] Baptist hath sent us unto thee, saying, Art thou he that should come? or look we for another? And in that same hour he cured many of their infirmities and plagues, and of evil spirits; and unto many that were blind he gave sight. Then Jesus answering said unto them, "Go your way, and tell John what things ye have seen and heard; how that the blind see, the lame walk, the lepers are cleansed, the deaf hear, the dead are raised, to the poor the gospel is preached. (Luke 7:18–22)

John the Baptist would have excited your imagination. First, there was the rugged, ascetic appearance and air of the man. His eyes were ablaze with a strange, intense fire, and his voice roared the judgment of God like peals of thunder, and his clothes were so different, exotic, strange, way out, actual camel's hair. Word drifted through the swank residential areas of Jerusalem that he ate the old diet of the desert, locusts and wild honey. This prophet, who held forth near the Jordan River, became the talk of the town. He was so picturesque, reminding the people of what they imagined the old prophets in Israel had been like. Some were deeply touched. Others were curious. But whatever the reason, one was not "in" in Jerusalem that season unless he had been out to the Jordan at least once to hear the preaching of John. People talked with a mixture of awe and respect and resentment of the things which this wilderness preacher was saying. His voice thundered about some impending judgment which hovered low and ominous like a cloud over the land. He talked about an "axe laid unto the root of the tree" and insisted that God was about to

---

Sermon delivered November 30, 1969.

86

do some new and mighty things. People, well, their task was to prepare the way of the Lord and to make straight in the desert a highway upon which the new adventure of God might proceed. John would make you almost tremble as he raised again the lyrics of Isaiah, "Every valley shall be filled, and every mountain and hill shall be brought low, and the crooked shall be made straight, and the rough way shall be made smooth, and all flesh shall see the salvation of God."

There was that day, many would never forget it, when Jesus showed up among John's hearers. Something instantly softened and surrendered in the grim, unflinching spirit of the wilderness preacher. He saw, he believed, the answer! He saw in Jesus the very visitation of God. "Behold the lamb of God," he cried, "who taketh away the sins of the world." It was like the coming of springtime after a long and biting winter. Jesus was the answer. All would be well.

But then John ran afoul of the vengeance of cruel King Herod and was thrown into a dismal, unlighted cell. He was not in despair. Hadn't he seen Jesus and discovered in him God's visitation? Soon the deliverer would strike the blow that would bring the year of jubilee. Down the unlighted cell block, rushing feet would be heard racing, and the rusty doors would creak as they were thrown open to let John out into the sunlight again, a free man. Jesus would do it, only he didn't. Caged in his prison, it is hard to imagine the questions which began to plague the mind of John. Did Jesus know? He must have heard what happened. Why didn't he do something then? At first he would smother the thought in his mind, ashamed of it. His plight, the silence of Jesus, long hours to brood, combined to make the question in John's mind too achingly sharp to be stifled any longer. "Hope deferred maketh the heart sick," wrote a wise man. And John's heart began to grow sick with doubt.

Is it that way with you? Heaven knows, you have tried to live a decent life, but things have turned out so poorly for you. You are imprisoned in ugly, terrifying conditions which you have done so little to deserve. Locked in sickness or imprisoned with family responsibilities which really belong to someone else, jailed by a dead end on the job, day after day you must get up to go through the old routine of quiet desperation. Night after night you stare into the darkness and stifle a sob and wonder deep down in your heart why God doesn't do something about it. If not so trapped, you and I ought to try to brace ourselves for those fearsome times when there is no light around us and the night of despair closes in upon us almost like choking fingers. A person can lose one's faith in the darkness if he or she is not careful and prayerful. Once I talked with a man by lovely Lake Geneva at the National Council of Churches assembly ground. He was a church executive, and in the gloaming he told me how in one year he lost his father, his wife, and his son. And then he said, "My grip nearly slipped." Sometimes in the darkness and the cold a person's grip will slip.

What is one to do then? What can one do? I like what John did as his grip of confidence in Jesus nearly slipped in the darkness of his prison cell. He did not conclude that all was hopeless and therefore there was no use attempting to do anything about the situation which wrenched his spirit and stuck in his heart like a dull, rusty sword. He decided to put the matter before the Master. John sent his friends to Jesus to report to him the anguished question which was tormenting the man in his prison cell. They sought an audience with Jesus and reported John's mood to him. "Our friend and former leader is in jail," they said. "His voice which once roared like thunder by Jordan's stream has been silenced by a vindictive king. He believed in you, and when you came to Jordan our teacher and leader, John, stepped out of the way saying that you, Jesus, must increase and he, John, must decrease. A long time now he has waited to hear in you footfalls of God's visitation to his people, Israel. He has believed that from you glorious tidings of deliverance would ring like stirring music through the land. But you have not been to see him, and you have not delivered him, and Israel still seems waiting for her redemption. Now, John has asked us to put the question to you bluntly. Art thou he that should come, the deliverer, the blessed of God? Or must we go back to the long, painful waiting for one who is come to set captive Israel free? "Art thou he, or should we look for another?"

Jesus' answer is characteristic, for God will not be put on trial. He is the judge of all the earth, and is not the defendant. He does not whine or beg. He states his case but does not wheedle or apple polish or grovel. God pleads, but always with the note of one who is in command. And so Jesus sent a word back to the lonely, tormented prisoner which was neither yes nor no but which was far more. "Tell John what you have seen and heard. Tell John the blind see, the lame walk, the lepers are cleansed, the deaf hear, the dead are raised. To the poor the gospel is preached. Tell him to make his decision upon the basis of my record."

You and I may have cried out ever so desperately, only never to receive the answer we want. Look around now and you will see, I think, in your life signs that God is at work, though not as you requested. When we are ready to conclude that there is no God anywhere and hope is dead, we ought to consider how it has been with us in the past, through what difficulties we have somehow been led. If a soul must doubt God's goodness, let him first feel the warming sun on a cold and chilly day. If one must doubt God's providence and protection, let him first think of the dangers through which the soul has been led, as if by another hand. If a woman must doubt God's goodness and kindness, let her first remember the blessings that have been in her path and the ways that have opened before her. If a man doubts God's judgment, let him look first at history and see a steady, unyielding pressure upon people to fashion a fair world or suffer the guilt and turmoil of an unjust one. I think there is abundant evidence that there is a purpose and a mercy operating in your life and in the world. Do you remember the words of a well-loved and steadying hymn,

> All the way my Savior leads me —
> What have I to ask beside?
> Can I doubt His tender mercy,
> Who thru life has been my Guide?
> Heav'nly peace, divinest comfort,
> Here by faith in Him to dwell!
> For I know, whate'er befall me,
> Jesus doeth all things well.

So to present to God whatever it is that troubles us and to cry out against it if need be, is our right as his people. Nor does it matter how bitter the complaint! Never forget the old psalm, "He knoweth our frame and remembereth that we are dust." There are days when we can bring before God a deep and glad laughter of joy and gratitude. There will be other days when we can only muster a bitter, angry complaint. If it is honest, be confident that God will accept whatever it is we truly have to lift up before him, and he will make it serve his purpose and our good.

A Sermon about Failure

Numbers 13:31–33

But the men that went up with him said, We be not able to go up against the people; for they are stronger than we. And they brought up an evil report of the land which they had searched unto the children of Israel, saying, The land, through which we have gone to search it, is a land that eateth up the inhabitants thereof; and all the people that we saw in it are men of a great stature. And there we saw the giants, the sons of Anak, which come of the giants: and we were in our own sight as grasshoppers, and so we were in their sight. (Numbers 13:31–33)

In the epic exodus of the Israelite slaves from Egypt, the weary wanderers came at last to the end of the desert journey, beyond what Moses had called that "waste howling wilderness." Encamped on Canaan's borders, with only the Jordan to cross, the Israelites had to decide whether they were ready to commit themselves to the final, bold push. It was their moment of decision.

Is it not true that we are always passing through various scenes and shifting circumstances? And does it not seem that these little experiences build up like some giant symphonic theme to a final moment of decision? In the Spanish bullfights the decisive time is called the moment of truth. It is the time when a final stroke must be made. On the other hand, the Greeks called the time of readiness *kairos*, the fullness of time, that mystic moment when all that one has been and is and hopes to be must be flung into the balance for better or for worse. Shakespeare sensed this peculiar, momentous time of decision which all of us know, and spoke of it as that gathering of events which produces the readiness of the tide to bear our frail hopes on to their golden port of destiny. Remember the familiar words, "There is a tide in the affairs of

---

Sermon delivered December 7, 1969.

men, when taken at the flood leads on to victory. Omit it, all the voyage of their life is bound in shallows and in miseries."

Let me venture a word about our country and its capacity to make decisions. The inability to make a moral commitment clearly and decisively and promptly and to stick by it may be the major weakness in this nation's character, with all of its other abundant, affirmative qualities. People may one day search for the reason why so great a nation as ours did not rise to lasting greatness. If this unhappy and unwelcome possibility happens, I believe they will say that here was a grand and prosperous people. One thing they lacked: the capacity to seize promptly the initiative in a right cause and to make whatever sacrifice, over however long a period necessary, to bring that decision to a successful issue.

Somber as it sounds, American history seems to support the thesis that an otherwise gallant and in many ways generous people appear to suffer from the serious weakness of undue reluctance, of letting well enough alone, reacting rather than initiating determined, sustained efforts to set right things that are wrong. We are accused of being a brash people, but in our great group commitments this may not be true at all. In the first great war, we hesitated before commitment and then, at the last, fell back in moral weariness from participation in the League of Nations, which with American participation might have been a mighty force for the abolition of the scourge of war. In the second great war, we waited until so much of Europe lay under the harsh hand of Nazi tyranny. After the Civil War, when so many Americans, North and South, had paid so great a price, testing, so to speak, in their own blood, the direction the nation would take, the same weakness of indecision of stamina seemed to seize the nation. After so great a cost of human life and the land violently torn in two, the nation could not bring itself to make unequivocal decision that this would be a nation of equals. With what tragic results we are all too familiar.

To see the right and to seize it and to serve it no matter the cost is God's mandate to this great and blessed land. How a soul bears itself at those crossroads of decision determines the difference between success and failure. Let me suggest that there are three reasons why so many of us are failures in life's testing warfare at the moment and place where faithful and far-reaching decisions must be made in our lives. They are, one, a faulty outward look; two, a faulty inward look; and three, a faulty upward look.

Now let us look again at Israel. Encamped on Canaan's borders, a sensation of excitement, mixed with dread, moves through the assembly like an electric current. All of the long journey has been building up to this moment. What would they do? Moses commissioned twelve men, representing the twelve tribes of Israel, to go forth on a mission of reconnaissance. They were to survey the land as to its desirability and were to assess the strength and weakness of those who dwelt in the land. All of this was with a view as to whether Israel would take the one last bold decisive step and go on over Jordan to claim Canaan as the land of promise.

They went forth, all saw the same land, and all viewed the same inhabitants. Ten brought back a report which doomed Israel to another forty years of homeless wandering in the desert. Two, Caleb and Joshua, brought back a minority report, "we are able." These latter two lost the vote, but they won God's good word, and they alone of that whole generation would enter the land of promise. Because of fear and defeatism, all of that crowd except Caleb and Joshua were condemned of God. He said to Moses, "Because all those men which have seen my glory and my miracles which I did in Egypt and the wilderness and have not hearkened to my voice, surely they shall not see the land which I swear unto their fathers. Your carcasses shall fall in this wilderness, save Caleb the son of Jephunneh, and Joshua the son of Nun. But your little ones, which ye said shall be prey, them will I bring in, and they shall know the land which ye have despised."

If you ask what was the reason for this failure, let us look at what happened. The spying party had a wrong outward look. They magnified the situation which they faced. There would be two reports, the majority report and the minority. Let the difference in the reports forever rebuke the notion that whatever the majority wants guarantees rightness. The admission was made by the majority that Canaan was a goodly land. They brought back pomegranates and figs and a great bunch of grapes swinging on a pole. Quickly they report this, and then start an account of how huge and unconquerable are the people who dwell in the land. The majority had gone to look for dangers, and they found them. At first they said that there were different groups beyond Jordan, some of them being the sons of Anak, a tall and formidable people. Later they get carried away with their own melancholy report and declared that all people they saw were of great stature. "And there we saw the giants," they reported.

So many of us always see the giants in our problems and difficulties. The job is too big, the odds are too huge. Now, we ought not to minimize what we face in life. We ought to take a true account of what the odds are. We ought to look at the situation honestly. But it is a faulty outward look only to see giants. Few situations in life are as bad as we make them, as frightening as we report them. We tend to enjoy making good things bad and bad things worse and talking about the negatives. A faulty outward look in your life will produce failure. If you believe that what you are up against in life is too much for you to meet and match and master, even with God's help, then you are already defeated.

These spies looked faultily at what was around them and then looked wrongly at themselves. Having convinced themselves that their enemies were invincible, these craven, cowardly reporters convinced themselves that they were grasshoppers. As they magnified the opposition they minimized themselves. They said, "And we were in our own sight as grasshoppers." Now, some of us have more advantage than others, but none of us is a grasshopper. There are talents in all of us. Everybody has something to offer that the world needs, if it is nothing more than a pleasant smile and an encouraging word. Indeed, I know of very little the world needs so much as these small signs of friendly interest. Every person must take what he is and what he has and make, by God's grace, something good enough and decent enough for him one day to hold it up before God unashamed.

Edward Bernays, the nephew of Sigmund Freud and one of the pioneers of the public relations enterprise, has written a long and detailed autobiography. In it he tells of his public relations service to a well-known jeweler. Mr. Bernays says that this jeweler longed to be an ambassador of his nation, France I believe, but his social station closed that career. What did he do? The frustrated would-be ambassador turned jeweler and made his jewelry business an example of old-world diplomacy, with elaborate secret codes and ceremonies attending the sale of merchandise. The manner the jeweler borrowed from his desire to be a diplomat made his firm rich and famous throughout the world. God gives us a little talent, or much, and a few years and some obstacles and tells us to make a life.

These men guaranteed failure by taking a faulty upward look. They had had dealings with God. They were witnesses to the safe passage of the Passover. They should have looked up and remembered that God lives and leads his people. They were men who had seen the waters of the Red Sea back up. They should have looked up and remembered. They miscalculated the strength of God. When the storms rise and headwinds blow biting in our faces, we ought to look up. A man is on his way to victory when he resolves, "I will lift up mine eyes unto the hills." When the storms are raging, we ought to lift up our eyes and, remembering what God has done for us in the past, press resolutely forward. In the day of battle when the tide rages and our very spirits faint within us and it seems that at every moment we will go down to crushing defeat, ought we not to look up and remember that "the LORD is my light and my salvation; whom shall I fear? The LORD is the strength of my life; of whom shall I be afraid?"

∽ 18 ∾

LIVING WITH CHANGE

Isaiah 40:6–8

The voice said, Cry. And he said, What shall I cry? All flesh is grass, and all the goodliness thereof is as the flower of the field: The grass withereth, the flower fadeth: because the spirit of the LORD *bloweth upon it: surely the people are grass. The grass withereth, the flower fadeth: but the word of our God shall stand forever. (Isaiah 40:6–8)*

There seems to be instinctive in us a desire for permanence, constancy, stability. Something in us seems to resist all change. This characteristic is baffling, since it does not grow out of our experience. The environmental psychologists would have to blink and stammer at this one. They say to us that we are the products totally of our experiences. Well, we have never known anything in this world that lasted. Each moment and minute of time has been a stern summons to keep moving. Time marches on, or is it down, or up? We have ever been on the march, living with change every day of our mortal journey.

Still, we long desperately for permanence and stability. Is it that we are really native to some other clime, originally citizens of some dispensation where shift and change are strange and alien? "Where all o'er those wide extended plains shines one eternal day." Do we come here by way of long human memory from some place where life and circumstance are unthreatened? Where "no chilling winds, no poisonous breath can reach that healthful shore, sickness and sorrow and pain and death are felt and feared no more." Was Wordsworth on truth's target when he said, "Trailing clouds of glory do we come from God who is our home"?

Whatever the case, we have to live with change. There are various versions of an instructive little story. One account of this

Sermon delivered December 14, 1969.

widely told tale's origin has it that Warren Hastings related it to some friends at the time of his trial in England. A monarch, so the tale runs, who suffered many hours of discouragement urged his courtiers to devise a motto short enough to be engraved on a ring, which should be suitable alike in prosperity and adversity. After many suggestions had been rejected, his daughter offered an emerald bearing the inscription in Arabic: "This, too, shall pass away." And so, whatever it is, it shall. We must learn to live with change.

Isaiah spoke in his lovely musical fortieth chapter of the transitoriness of all that is on earth as over against the unchangeableness of God. Israel was enduring a bitter slavery. Her oppressors seemed invulnerable and unconquerable. Babylon had built a mighty empire. Her star in its ascendancy seemed so bright that it could never decline in brilliance and power. The downcast and dispirited exiles by Babylon's streams could not help feeling overawed and forever helpless in the face of the great military juggernaut and the economic colossus which held them as slaves in the iron grip of its powerful hand.

As they looked around at the splendor of the architecture and masonry of Babylon, these slaves must have felt very small and insignificant. These poor Israelite captives had seen the wondrous hanging gardens of Babylon, called one of the wonders of the ancient world. Tradition says that these hanging gardens were composed of trees and flowers planted upon terraces, one upon the other, to a height of one hundred fifty feet and watered by means of a device similar to an invention of Archimedes. The humble, ill-clad slaves looking at this dazzling sight must have felt a terrible despair and an aching longing for home. Their melancholy cry cuts at the heart as they lamented. "By the waters of Babylon, there we sat down, yea, we wept, when we remembered Zion." The society among which they were aliens and slaves was so highly developed and so intricately accomplished in literature and commerce and business. Modern excavations reveal an amazing body of literature carefully catalogued like a modern library. Babylon's tax structure was elaborate and sophisticated, and her deeds and mortgages and bills of sale attest to a highly developed

culture. What could some slaves mean midst all these achievements when they had only some exotic ways of worship and an
invisible God upon whom to call midst the galling yoke and heavy
oppression of their captivity?

The unknown prophet of the exile whom we call Isaiah took
one look at all of this heathen splendor and pagan power and
saw the fatal void at the heart of it all. Isaiah saw a deep and
awful night, unillumined by the true and living God, at the very
center of the bright achievements of Babylon culture. The prophet
saw the mighty architecture of Babylonian power, unsupported
by the Rock of Ages but erected upon shifting sand and treacherous soil. His voice rises like a trumpet of doom and hope midst
the scattered dreams and sagging morale of God's own people.
"All flesh is grass, and all the goodliness thereof is as the flower
of the field."

"Never mind," he must have mused, "how green and lush the
grass may seem. Never mind how bright and picturesque the
blossoming flowers may appear." Then he went on, "The grass
withereth, the flower fadeth." Let every person who stands in failure or success take note of this word. In the hour of failure we are
likely to feel that all is lost, that we have come upon some endless desert, and for us there is no deliverance. People's hearts in
such hours fail them with fear. It takes a mighty courage to keep
on marching when the journey seems endless and the pilgrimage
seems hopeless. We can bear almost anything — personal misfor-
tune, sickness, injustice, poverty, whatever — as long as we have
some assurance as to when and how it will end. The sword passes
to the heart when trudging a weary and rough way we see no sign
of relief, no end, not even a turning. It is then that we are likely
to feel a deep, numbing despair.

A gasp of admiration crosses the spirit when we think of people
who have been able to look through their fears and peer through
their heartbreak to the faith that nothing in this world remains
the same. "I'm so glad trouble don't last always," some people
desperately circumstanced once said, and found bright dawn for
their deep night. On the other hand, the man who stands in
the heady moment of success needs to hear the prophet's words.

When things go well with us, we tend to believe that the sun will always shine. Of course, we ought not to be constantly looking for a blow to fall, for sober tidings which snatch the breath away and leave us stunned and gasping. At the same time, in the day of calm, we ought while enjoying the quiet beauty, set ourselves for the time of storm and fury. We want our high and happy moments to go on forever. We do not want our privileged status in society changed. We want always to be praised and lauded and honored. We do not want to see our neighborhoods change. We want our church to remain the same. This a vain longing.

Change is the law of our lives, and we cannot maintain anything as we would have it. We are sailing on a restless sea. The voyage does not remain the same. We are going forward, or we are driven back. White-capped waves dash to and fro. There is endless, restless change on this bounding tempestuous sea. There are no permanent markers. The moon pulls at the sea, and the winds whip the waters. How shall we steer? By what shall we mark our way?

To change the prophet's figure but not his truth, look up. Midst all this change there is a star. It is the North Star. For those who live in the northern hemisphere, the Pole Star is the one heavenly light which does not change position. The old sailors sailed by it. Wind and sun and moon and constellations shifted, but the North Star stayed in place. Even now the navigator must test his compass by the reliable constancy of the North Star.

Quickly now, do you see the answer to the whole thing? How odd of us not to notice that there is an answer, sure and certain, to our longing for abidingness. It really does not need any comment from me. "The grass withereth, the flower fadeth; but the word of our God shall stand for ever." There, there is your North Star. Steer carefully and steadily by it.

⁓ 19 ⁓

THE CHRISTMAS MYSTERY

Luke 2:8–14

And the angel said unto them, Fear not: for, behold, I bring you good tidings of great joy, which shall be to all people. For unto you is born this day in the city of David a Savior, which is Christ the Lord. (Luke 2:10–11)

The time of singing has come, for it is the Christmas season again. The old mystery has happened once more, and the hardness drops strangely from our hearts. The ice leaves our eyes, and the fire of human warmth and understanding burns there instead. It is Christmas again, and the countenance loses it frigidness and stoniness and becomes wreathed in smiles and human interest. A lilt is in the land and a song is on the air. Christmas is a time of mystery. The world becomes suddenly, and for a while, fresh again, and eyes long accustomed to squinting with suspicion for a while open in honest surprise and gladness. The least spiritually sensitive person among us senses that what Christmas celebrates is something far and away beyond the ordinary. Mystery, a strange, inexplicable event whose meaning we cannot fully discern, transpires at Christmas. Christ is born! Something new, decisive, winsome, wonderful, redeeming has occurred. Christ is born! And knowing little of the theological terms, we feel God is near. Oh, surely we recognize and admit the human trimmings, the tinsel and trees, the carols and candy, the laughter of children and the singing of choirs, but underneath it all there lies something else, the Christmas mystery.

It was ever so as on that first unforgettable day when Christ was born. There were the elements of mystery, strange, baffling. There was the mystery of infancy. The supreme word of God's arrival did not declare that a bejeweled emperor had come among

---

Sermon delivered December 21, 1969.

the daughters and sons of the earth with a glittering court of witty lords and well-dressed ladies, but rather the word was, "Ye shall find the babe wrapped in swaddling clothes and lying in a manger." No earthly silver trumpet sounded. No drums played. No armies marched. No political scepters changed hands on that first Christmas, for it was the mystery of infancy. "For unto you a child is born, for unto you a son is given." The mystery of infancy is the mystery of God giving a fresh start and out of oldness bringing newness. This is the promise of every child.

I suppose that there has been one statement repeated more often than any other in the deprived homes of this land by parents in hut and hovel, on vast plantation and in crowded slum. That statement, over all these years, and rising out of the most discouraging and painful disadvantage and penalty has been, "I want my child to have a better chance than I had." Yes, and if there is a thrilling saga of human development in this land, it has been because people believe that their children represent something fresh and hopeful and bright, not bound by the old past.

The mystery of infancy is the mystery of newness and of birth. God's power is not exhausted, every child's life says. This is the mystery of a child. She or he comes forth from parents whose bones are hardened, whose habits are formed, whose mindsets are pretty well fixed, and whose thought patterns are established. But the baby is a new creature, with all the vast possibilities of far horizons and distant vistas stretching infinitely before him or her. That child, any child, might inaugurate a new era in the history of the world. There may be in any nursery this morning, maybe the one in your house, a little life now that will one day lift the heavy hand of cancer from the human race, or open the gates of new liberty and dignity to all sons and daughters of earth. For the mystery of a child is the mystery of new beginning. God's power is not exhausted, a child's life says, but righteousness can blossom where sin and ugliness have lived.

The birth of Jesus heralds the arrival of a new chance for the children of the world. He is the way to a new birth and to a new life. He offers to humanity a fresh start. He is empowered to say, "Thy sins be forgiven," to make it right between us and God, to pull down the middle wall of partition, to bid us to be reconciled. "If any man be in Christ, he is a new creature."

Christmas proclaims, alas, the mystery of iniquity also. Amidst angels, anthems, and a bright star, sin reared its ugly head and sin spoke its loathsome word when Christ was born. Herod inserted his vulgar ambitions and ugly deceptions into the blessed entrance of God among humanity. Herod heard, says Matthew, that a child had been born or was to be born whose future threatened the wily old king's future. Whenever righteousness appears, unrighteousness is challenged and threatened. So Herod is represented as pressing the wise men for details as to where the young child could be found, and then advanced as his reason for wanting to know the location because he desired to worship the Christ child.

Thus, to the mystery of infancy we must add the mystery of iniquity. From whence did it come? God, in the completion of creation, ruled out the possibility that sin could have entered as a by-product of his own creative acts. Sin was not the debris, the trash left from God's creative labors, for God himself looked around over all that he had made and said, "It is good." Yet, by some mystery, iniquity is with us. A gloomy religionist in Israel felt that this perversity so much pervades and permeates life, is so woven into the fiber and stuff of our humanity that he could say that we are born in sin and shaped in iniquity. Sin is with us. No small palliatives, no cute cures, no mild remedies will banish it. Against the power of evil we must make war every day, for Satan goes forth to and fro seeking whom he may devour, the Scriptures assert. We must fight the war against sin, personal and public, all our lives, and renew the battle every day. We have a right to celebrate the joys and gladness of Christmas time. But we have no right to let the tinsel and turkey and trimmings blind us to the truth that there is much that is ugly in the plight of our cities. There is much that is evil and sinful in the disparities among us that allow some to have so much in this country while others live their lives in the shadow of hunger and poverty and squalor. Christmas declares that even when God does his best, iniquity arises and begins peddling its wares and transacting its business. Christmas shows us the mystery of stubborn iniquity.

Christmas supremely declares the mystery of God's invasion of our little time sphere. Men have recurringly felt and feared that God was far removed from the pygmy affairs of the sons and daughters of earth, did not have time to be bothered. Some wove a philosophy out of the idea that God was prime mover, and then, when he started time to run and worlds to roll, resigned from active participation. But Christmas says that God has never given up on the world. Even at its worst, God is interested, so interested that he identifies himself with us. In all their affliction he was afflicted. The mystery baffles us but wins us. The working out of the life of the Christ child was so momentous, and the impact of that life was so great upon people and upon history that they who knew him best and were closest to him were forced to account for him on other than merely human grounds. They sensed in him the very presence of the divine. With his birth, the eternal had got inside of time, and God had come among men and women as one of them in the ultimate act of identification and love. Christmas is our evidence that far from abandoning the world, God has visited it in Jesus Christ, entering into the heat and sweat and sorrow and pain and death and of it all. This is the glorious good news of Christmas, the best news the world has ever known.

Indeed, it is so wonderful one can understand how we find it incredible, unbelievable, but there it all is, there in the Christmas gospel. There it is, all implicit in the Bethlehem birth. So sound the glad sound of music. Let every heart rejoice. "Joy to the world, the Lord is come, let earth receive her King. Let every heart prepare him room, and heaven and nature sing."

⌒ 20 ⌒

AT YEAR'S END

Psalm 55:22

Cast thy burden upon the LORD, and he shall sustain thee: he shall never suffer the righteous to be moved. (Psalm 55:22)

Thoughtless indeed must be the person who does not think a little more seriously at the turning of the year. People of sane mind will feel a compulsion to reflect soberly and solemnly at a time like this. At year's end we think of the road over which we have come, the fulfillments, the disappointments, the successes, the failures. We think of those whose physical presence is faded from gaze during the twelvemonth gone, the sicknesses that were upon us, the deliverances we experienced, the dangers seen and unseen. In so looking back, we cannot help wondering at two things. First, we are amazed at how easy things were that at first looked difficult, if not impossible. One shakes his head unbelievingly at how that chasm that could not be crossed, or so it seemed, was crossed, and with what ease. We remember also that we did not possess any sudden new knowledge that got us safely through. It was too easy to be due to what we did. I think serious reflection will drive us to declare that the way we have come was not our doing at all. I think at year's end the sentiment of a rejoicing singer in ancient Israel will be on our tongues and in our hearts: "This is the LORD's doing; it is marvelous in our eyes."

While these musings throw their lights and shadows across our minds and our memories we are aware of a certain embarrassment at year's end. We could have made the last year so much better for ourselves, and indeed for all around us if we had tried a little harder. We let down too often, we can see that, and failed to give our best, and now it is past and the opportunity is gone.

Sermon delivered December 28, 1969.

We let subtle siren voices within whisper the wrong advice, fool us, and deceive us. It's over now, and we can't call it back.

What shall we do at year's end? Well, there was a psalmist in Israel whose name we do not know but with whose case we are all intimately familiar. Reverses have been upon him. His soul has been shaken under the most painful blows. He feels helpless, frustrated, spent. Sometimes he has fancied the idea of giving up, of letting go and letting down. A portion of the fifty-fifth psalm is one of the classic laments of the Bible. It pictures a soul at wit's end, ready to throw in the towel, to haul up the white flag of surrender. Listen: "Oh that I had wings like a dove! for then would I fly away, and be at rest." But then his faith in God speaks to the conditions that pain and taunt him, and he comes forward with the loftiest decision of religious faith. "Cast your burden on the Lord, and he will sustain you. He shall never permit the righteous to be moved."

At year's end we have the burden of lost opportunities. "Looking back," as Nat Cole used to sing, we see how we could have made things better for ourselves, but even more so for those around us. No matter who we are, how humble our status, we have the power to make things a little better or a little worse for those we know. I think this is a significant and incalculably important asset that belongs to us. You can actually throw a little sunshine on another life for which Christ thought enough to be born and to die. Or, conversely, you can darken the day of such a one. Trustee of someone's happiness, that's what you are. God has made you so. A sharp tongue, an impudent word, a selfish spirit in you, and at year's end you know you failed in that opportunity. There was the opportunity to make your life count for God and good in a word about what the Lord has done in your life to that groping, wandering friend who does not know your Lord.

It would be a glorious day for the things of God if his people would recapture the first strategy of Jesus for the spread of the good news of the kingdom. It all started as a word-of-mouth campaign, issuing out of the experience of Christ, which men knew in their regular, everyday lives. Back and forth through the alleys and streets of the towns of Galilee, up and down the roads of the empire, they passed on the good news of Jesus Christ by word of mouth, fully believing that all the world must know and then rejoice that Jesus has been here. Good gossip about God's goodness is the missing note among us.

At year's end, we think also of how swiftly time is getting away from us. It hardly seems possible that a whole year has gone, and yet it has. We wish we could call the time back and bring again the green years. It seems so short a time when we stood with all of our years before us, bright, shining, hopeful. There was so much to be done, and we were bright-eyed with eagerness about our power to get the deal done, to build a good life for ourselves and our children and, yes, to make the world better because we dreamed "the impossible dream." Today the years have sped by, and we are cut off from another twelve months. We never had a chance to get set. There was one thing after another and, well, time slipped away. How long do we have left? Authentic wishfulness is to be found in the hymn "Time like an ever rolling stream bears all its sons away. They fly forgotten as a dream dies at the opening day."

At year's end, there is the burden of not just missed chances, passing years, but of open, downright clear-cut mistakes we have made. There was a fork in the road, and we took the wrong turn. There was a decision to be made, and we reached the wrong one. We spoke too fast or not fast enough and now it's done, our fate is sealed. I think the psalmist's word ought to speak to us: "Cast thy burden upon the LORD, and he shall sustain thee." We cannot get the year back again, but the Lord can make our failures and mistakes, our lost opportunities and our muffed chances turn out to his name's glory and to our own strengthening. It is the glory of our faith that the Lord will sustain those who put their faith in him.

A British chaplain in the late war tells of a terrible day when a regiment was about to move out to what looked like a fearfully hazardous and maybe fatal mission. The night before they sailed, a vaudeville company was entertaining the regiment. During the lull in the performance, a young soldier with the fear of death in his voice stood and asked, "Is there anybody here who can tell me how to die?" A lovely girl in the troupe stood and calmly sang that haunting aria from Mendelssohn's *Elijah*, "Oh, rest in the Lord, wait patiently for him, and he will give thee thy heart's desire." It is more than a song, it is very truth. The Lord will sustain those who put their trust in him. Our errors may have been many this dying year. A mood of regret might and ought to fill our hearts, for we have not done what we should have done, and we have not been what we should have been. In godly sorrow, in humble repentance, we can cast our cares upon the Lord, and he will sustain us, releasing us from the burden of guilt about past failure and sending us forth strong in the strength of those who move in the power of the eternal God.

The good news of the gospel is that we have another chance. How futile and barren life would be if this were not the case. With our errors and our mistakes, our perverse and stubborn preference for the wrong decisions, or so it seems, our days on the earth would be shrouded in despair, except for this one rallying asset. We sense when we are most ourselves a presence, assuring us that we have not been abandoned but are still counted as trusted children and heirs. So, there is a dignity in our days, and there is a sure sense of the royal order to which we belong as the sons and daughters of God. Cast your burdens upon him.

ᘒ 21 ᘓ

Soul for Sale

Matthew 16:26

For what is a man profited, if he shall gain the whole world, and lose his own soul? or what shall a man give in exchange for his soul? (Matthew 16:26)

The man who doubts the integrity of all other men is likely to say that every man has his price, meaning of course that a person's loyalty or love or support can be bought. Such a verdict puts a person's soul, his essential honor and character and being, on a level of houses and land and other transferable commodities. We expect to see signs on houses which say "for sale," and we are not shocked when we see "for sale" signs on automobiles. We are dismayed at the thought of a price tag on a person walking down the street. Our nation has never gotten over the degrading bitterness of slavery. Perhaps there was nothing more debasing about slavery than the idea of human beings on auction blocks. A revulsion sweeps through us when we see pictures of men and women and children being examined and bought like horses or cattle, but even slavery could not buy and sell the soul. There is abundant evidence that many in the cruel clutches of the slave trader still retained their essential integrity and personhood. While not even slavery could contract the sale of the soul, each of us had better hear the words of Jesus, for some of us are selling our souls too cheaply.

Charlemagne, the wise and benevolent ruler of the Franks, reigned forty-six years and left a record of loyalty to faith and to education. When he died, this wise and honored king was not buried as if sleeping in his shroud in a reclining position; rather he was buried seated on a throne in robes of state with an open Bible on his knee, one dead cold finger pointed to the words of

Sermon delivered January 18, 1970.

Jesus that live on when kings are dead and empires are dust. "For what is a man profited if he shall gain the whole world and lose his own soul?"

Now every person is for sale. It is a matter of for what or how much. We are negotiable. We may attempt to stand on dead center doing no business in loyalty and allegiance and love, stubbornly trying to be completely neutral, but neutrality is not our natural estate. No one can assume neutrality in the real or the physical world, for instance, by saying, "I will neither eat nor fail to eat. I will be neutral," or "I will neither breathe nor fail to breathe. I will be neutral." As in the physical so in the spiritual we are made to be used, to love and to be loved, to spend and to be spent. The matter is not whether our souls are to be claimed or owned by somebody or something else. The question is rather by whom or what. Yes, our souls are for sale.

In order to find out whether they are bringing a fair price we ought to examine the commodity. What is a human soul? How do we measure its worth? A human soul is the totality of our personhood. It is the essential "I" and "you" with all the wrappings pulled away. We are, beneath flesh and bone, persons who love and hate, who worship and work, who respond to God and to humanity, who dream and dare. How much is that worth? Well, we need to examine a little more who we are before we set a price tag on ourselves. I take it that what we call the most ordinary person is an amazing and fantastic wonder. Have you ever considered that God has fixed you so that there never has been another you? Never your identical likeness in the long sweep of history. There never was another you with the same emotional balance, the exact talents or a precisely similar mind and imagination, no, and there never will be another you. If the world is to go on for another millennium or ten the world will never again see your exact duplicate.

Even more important than this vastly astonishing truth is the fact that God has dealt with us. Each of us is made in the image of God so that deep down underneath there is an essential likeness to God in us, an instinct toward righteousness underneath our proneness to evil and wrong, an instinct toward holiness

underneath our tendency to profane and defame our life. "Know
ye not that ye are the temple of God, and that the spirit of God
dwelleth in you?" This is what we are worth, and it is this truth
we must take into account when we ask the question: What shall
a man give in exchange for his soul?

Consider again our destiny. Every human person, like God, is
eternal. This is our faith. The persons we really are, are scheduled
to travel on beyond our flesh. This body will weaken and decay
and die, but our personhood, our soul quality is to go on and live
as long as God shall live. When mountains have crumbled and
the earth goes up in flames and the sky melts with fervent heat
our essential personhood is to continue. This is the blessed hope
of the Christian faith.

I submit to you in the light of this that too many of us sell
our souls too cheaply. There are men and women who place no
higher value upon their souls than a few dollars or some clothes
or a little earthly honor or somebody's praise. There is nothing
that perishes and rots which is a fair price in exchange for what
does not die. I must be honest for a moment, and if morbid in
order to be honest then make the most of it. All of the earthly
prizes and holdings that we have must be torn from our hands
by the passage of time and the clutch of death. All must go. The
fresh beauty of a young face fades with the wrinkles of the rapidly
moving years. The quick bouncy step is slowed by the weight of
passing time. Friends separate and kinfolk die. There are needs
of the soul which money cannot buy and yearnings which honors
cannot satisfy. Think now of the little things we settle for, a shiny
car out of style next week, a new fashion we would be ashamed to
be seen in next year, some little honor that turns to dust. Let the
width and breadth of the earthly prize vastly expand to whatever
dimension you can conceive and you know you are worth more
still than the baubles and prizes, the petty distinctions and false
values. Hear the word of Jesus as he asks, "What shall it profit a
man if he shall gain the whole world and lose his own soul?"

Midst the din and strife of our time nothing is clearer than the
truth that God is our only hope. All else is sinking sand. Gain
the whole world. What is it? I will tell you. The whole world

is a vast nervous disorder, apparently headed for flames and destruction. Modern science and human sinfulness have combined to pull the mask of splendor off this ugly doomed world. All of us smiled in a superior way at the old ideas of "wars and rumors of wars," of signs in the sun and the moon dripping in blood and the earth going up in smoke. Now we stand with the possibility of nuclear fate too horrible to imagine. The rocket juggling and missile waving going on in our world cast a long dark shadow over the future of the earth.

Let us not be too grim. Maybe the world's best days are on ahead. Still destruction edges near in one way or another. Trouble is in the air. I know of no shelter except Jesus Christ. He is the only hiding place from the tempest, the only shadow of a great rock in a weary land. Safe where? Safe nowhere except in the care and keeping of God. I hear people speak of dreadful possibilities who know the Lord, and what do they say? Well, one says of some cosmic replacement, "I saw a new heaven and a new earth," or another contemplating his own demise said, "But we know that if this earthly house is dissolved we have another building not made with hands, eternal in the heavens." What will a man give in exchange for his soul? There is nothing except God that is worth all that we are.

～ 22 ～

STRANGE INTERLUDE

Luke 3:1–2

. . . the word of God came unto John the son of Zacharias in the wilderness. (Luke 3:2)

There are sharp-corner turnings in human history on this planet. More often than not, those changes are announced by strange and apparently unimportant and isolated events. Not caused by those events, but declared by those events. For instance, on the twenty-eighth of June 1914, in the obscure town of Sarajevo in eastern Europe, an archduke was killed. That event heralded the beginning of the first great war, and the world was to be forever altered. New eras arrive almost unbelievably, and the direction history is about to take is an almost unfathomable mystery. Years ago I came very near the city of Troas, which lies in the northwestern part of Asia. The apostle Paul came to that city and looked back eastward toward Bithynia and Galatia. For so long the center of history had focused there. A vision came to him, he said, urging him to turn westward, toward Macedonia, and so the gospel moved westward up through Europe and out to the new world. Suppose Paul had turned eastward toward the Russian steppes bearing the precious seed of the gospel. What would have been the course of history?

New eras, new ages appear among men, and they do not come by human reckoning but by God's will. There is an incurable disease among human beings, especially those who at the moment are in power, which convinces them that they will continue in power forever. In Thomas Bailey's exhaustive work on our United States presidents, entitled *Presidential Greatness*, he quotes one of our presidents as anticipating the thousandth generation of Americans. What amazing self-assurance! We shall need to bring forth

---

Sermon delivered January 25, 1970.

better fruits for our repentance. A German leader's comment that God is on the side of the nation with the largest battalions should be judged in the light of what happened to him and his armies. God speaks in the language of events, and people find themselves made or broken by the side on which they stand.

Who would have given a plugged nickel in support of what John the Baptist stood for as over against the people who seemed to be in power? Luke seems to be deliberately stating how impossible was the case for this wilderness creature as he recites the time when John appeared in his public ministry. "The fifteenth year of the reign of Tiberius Caesar," and one immediately is aware of the purple of royalty, the invariably obeyed command of the emperor, armies, palaces, courtiers. "Pontius Pilate, being governor," and there occurs before the imagination the delegated authority of the second line of government. "Herod being tetrarch," and one senses the oriental splendor of an iniquitous king and his family moving in great luxury. If the air was foul and stifling in political circles, it was scarcely clearer or fresher in the church. "Annas and Caiaphas being the high priests," conniving politicians they were, dividing the immense power which went with religious authority. At first blush, you would think the writer has said all that can be said about authority and power and the future. The truth is that when he recites the list of these leaders of state and religion, the writer is only clearing ground for something important to which he wants to get. These rulers with all their fancied authority and regal splendor are a part of the scenery for something really momentous and important. "The Word of God came to John, the son of Zacharias, in the wilderness."

How odd of God to bypass the correct people and to speak to this crank in the wilderness. John did not fit the description of a reliable public figure. He lacked many of the expected features of an acceptable person. First, he was not as affable and social as a normal person should be. He lived in the solitude of the desert. He was a brooding man with strange wheels turning in his head, the fashionable people of Jerusalem said. His dress was odd, to say the least. The word was that he wore camel's hair, not the refined cloth which we call camel's, but the actual hair of the camel.

Now, every respectable person wore regular cloth. His diet, well, the rumor was that he ate the old food of the poor, locusts mixed with honey from bees. He was "way out." God marches among us in weird ways and puts the shout of his approach upon strange lips. Many of us are likely to be enraged by those who hear drumbeats, not audible to our ears, but which may be announcement of the future.

I know how distressed many older people are with many young people. What with their strange abruptness and peculiar styles of dress and life and, oh, surely, there is much wrong with them, not least of which is that arrogance which seems to be youth's disease and from which preceding generations have not been notably spared. At the same time, may it not be that many of these young people have caught hold of a special vision, distorted by their youthful optimism and oversimplification to be sure, but still a splendid vision? Perhaps they have seen accurately too many of the shams and pretenses of their elders, for heaven knows my generation lived so long, so comfortably with so much that was wrong in this country — poverty, hunger, racism, war.

I know as I look at John the Baptist and Elijah and Moses and Paul and, yes, Jesus, that the changes of God seldom come from nice people. So anxious to be proper they cannot be passionate. Now, there is a virtue in preserving the hard-won gains of the community. There must be some stable institutions which house and protect the best insights of the past.

We have in this country a lot of people who claim to be Christians and, in a sense, are, I suppose. But they are as far away from the fresh winds of God as one pole from the other. They want nothing but comfort in their religion. They can think of nothing more important than that something has been done a certain way all along. That kind of congregation dismisses its ministers and rejects the fellowship of its denomination because it does not want to be disturbed or to have mentioned to it what is wrong. Things like civil rights and all that. They want to hear only about peace of mind and the joy of salvation. To have such a mood is not necessarily fickle. Institutions and individuals may not be able to face up and to march boldly toward the future. They may be in love with the past, but they can, by God's grace and their own effort, serve the things of God; if they will midwife the future, offering deliverance for its ideas, tolerating the awkward business of the future's birth, they may still serve God. At the same time, the direction of God's purposes will not wait on our convenience or our agreement. The announcement that something new is about to take place will come. If the church will not trumpet it, the school will. If the school will not, the theater will or a man standing alone will.

God will be heard, and so a man named John in the wilderness was crazy enough to feel called of God, not to be a spokesman for his own small ideas. This is the curse of so many of our pulpits, but a spokesman for the everlasting God must articulate God's ideas. John was not in the business of echoing the popular clichés and moods of the day. The mighty pressures of God played upon his life. His words were swift and sharp like lightning. Clear and blazing like the noonday desert sun. He was not talking the petty wisdom distilled from the waters of his own observation, little scraps of human shrewdness. He saw mighty events, momentous anticipations of incredible things about to happen. The *kairos* had come, the moment of truth, of divine invasion was impending. A sharp and radical change was about to take place. There is an expectancy, natural and exciting, which comes to the true person of God. The everlasting God is not prisoner of what has already happened. Something new is about to take place. John saw it clearly. "Prepare ye the way of the Lord." Make his path straight. Every valley shall be exalted. Let low swamps of prejudice and passion and pettiness be lifted. Let cliffs of pride and haughtiness be leveled. Every mountain shall be brought low. This was what we can do. We cannot bring to pass the things God will have happen. We can open up the highways upon which his purposes might move. This our calling.

‿ 23 ‿

Shadow and Light

Isaiah 38:17

Behold, for peace I had great bitterness: but thou hast in love to my soul delivered it from the pit of corruption: for thou hast cast all my sins behind thy back. (Isaiah 38:17)

The photographer insists that his subject stand in front of a contrasting color, lest the wrong combination of shadow and light spoil the sharpness of the picture. If the person or object to be photographed is the same color and wears the same color apparel as the color of the background, the picture is ruined. This is an elementary fact of photography which ought, incidentally, to say something to our sick unwillingness to see blessing in the fact that we are white and black in this land.

Once, on a lovely summer's day, I visited the home of the painter Rembrandt in Amsterdam. The guide kindly suggested that those in our party should study the painter's work for the sharp quality of his shadows and light. That day, we saw the original Rembrandt painting entitled "The Night Watch." In it, one could see that the genius of Rembrandt, or at least a part of it, lay in the artistry with which he mixed his colors, so that actual shadows seemed to lurk on the canvas, over against which, by contrast, the bright objects take on what looked like an intense light, as if a high-powered incandescent bulb is shining on the subject. Women, of course, know about that in their decorative schemes, throwing dark and light colors in such combination as to bring out some particular brightness one wishes to achieve. Nature around us seems to support the idea of contrasting colors, for we see the arctic gloom of winter's chill season, which serves as a foil and preparation for the bright green mood of spring. One

---

Sermon delivered February 1, 1970.

sees the contrast of shadow and light in the incessant shift from daytime to nighttime and back again.

It is this strange dimension of both shadow and light in which we stand in our relationship to God. We are, as someone points out in a book, both under the shadow of God's judgment and under the light of God's grace. It is this awareness of both guilt and forgiveness, judgment and restoration, sorrow and joy, which gives to the life in God a peculiar quality which produces tears and laughter, heaviness and lightness of heart. When I contemplate my relationship with God, I feel sad, but I feel glad. There was a time when I could not understand this. As a lad, I used to see my elders in moments of great religious experience break down in tears. I wondered if they had found in Christ so much joy and peace, why they would cry. The years have taught their lesson. Thinking of what we have done against God and thinking of what God has done for us will melt the stoniest heart. Isaac Watts, contemplating the dark shadow of his guilt and the bright light of his dying Savior's love, has caught the meaning in ever-living melody.

> Alas, and did my Savior bleed,
> and did my Sovereign die?
> Would he devote that sacred head
> for such a worm as I?

> Thus might I hide my blushing face
> while his dear cross appears;
> Dissolve, my heart, in thankfulness!
> And melt, mine eyes, to tears!

We stand under the shadow of God's judgment.

In one place, the Bible asserts, "All have sinned and come short of the glory of God." There is no exception. The wisest person is sinner, as is the stupidest person. The proud moralist is as surely a sinner before God as is the most profligate worldling. "All have sinned." Someone says, "Well, that's what you think. But I've never considered myself bad, not really." That is beside the point. Imagine how many of us are carrying deadly disease every day who consider ourselves quite healthy. The point is that none of us is so good that we have kept God's law in our thoughts, in

our deeds, in the desires of our heart. We have done countless
acts of treason against the holiness of God's commands. We have
forsaken his way and have walked after our own wisdom. When
we think of what angry, bitter passions we and those like us have
loosed in the world, we are aware that we could not and cannot
approach God as we are.

I heard a Jewish leader of my community remind us again, not
long ago and rightly, that in Hitler's Germany, race prejudice destroyed the physical lives of six million Jews, while the rest of the
world scarcely raised a finger of protest. This is a kind of sickness,
though admittedly not to the same degree, that most of us show
in one form or another at one time or another. All have sinned.
There is this scarlet shadow over our nation. We may puzzle as
to why our nation is strained and torn at so many points. Race,
the generation chasm, class antagonism. Underneath the specifics
is almost always that old antagonist of the human soul and of
human society, selfishness. We continue to live "inward" instead
of "outward." We continue to worship things, to serve ourselves
rather than having ourselves serve what is worthy of our love
and loyalty. We continue to think of race in small selfish terms
of color or class or section, rather than in the broad terms of humanity and that sonship which is the birthright of all people. We
continue to think of human beings in terms of the narrow consid-
eration of chronology, of how old one is or how long the hair, of
what the style of clothing is, rather than in broad inclusive terms
of our common humanity. We continue to think about our great
national issues in terms of our own prejudices and preferences,
rather than as massive, puzzling problems to which we ought to
bring humility as well as conviction. In it all, one sees the attempt
to claim the partial as being the whole, to make self worthy of
that worship which belongs alone to God, the refusal to let "my"
become "our." This is partly what sin is all about.

At the very moment we stand under the shadow of God's judgment for our sins, we stand also in the light of his grace. Sinner?
Yes. Under the shadow of God's judgment, surely. But then it
must also be said that you stand in a great light. "Ye are a chosen
generation, a royal priesthood and holy nation, a peculiar people,

that ye should show forth the praises of him who has called you out of darkness into his marvelous light," so the Bible speaks. We stand in the light of his forgiveness. The debt for those who own Christ and are owned of him, who throw themselves on his mercy, is all wiped away. 'Tis a terrible load to carry the burden of unforgiven sin, to know that we are in unpardoned violation of God's holy law. But there is peace and there is joy in knowing that the debt is settled. The mark against us is moved, and one may be in good relationship with God again. When God forgives, every shadow of shame and guilt passes away. Years ago, I used to hear the old people pray, "Cast our sin in the sea of forgetfulness, where it will never rise against us in this world and neither condemn us at your just bar." I did not know that there was any actual basis for so fond a hope. But thanks be to God, there is.

It is written in the volume of the Book of Books, God is talking: "Though your sins be as scarlet, they shall be as white as snow. Though they be red like crimson, they shall be as wool." Someone says that this is not getting rid of the shadow fully enough. Then hear God again. "I am he," cries Jehovah God, "I am he that blotteth out thy transgressions." Or hear again, a forgiven man crying to God: "Thou hast in love to my soul delivered it from the pit of corruption: for thou hast cast off my sins behind thy back." Oh, the wild, glad exuberant language of the forgiven! Dare this man to say that God has put what was between him and his Maker behind the Lord's back? What glorious nonsense is this? There is no knowledge behind God, and yet this is precisely what this man is saying. That one whose sins are forgiven has had them put where not even God sees them any longer. Those who are so forgiven walk in the light of his love. The shadows are passed away. The clouds are faded away. The storm has passed over. The way grows brighter. Faith shines clearer. God becomes more real as we walk in the light of his grace. Deep may be the night, but there is a light that shines for God's people, shines more brightly as the night deepens and thickens. And there is in this light of God's forgiveness a sense that all is well. Naught can defeat us or destroy us.

✂ 24 ✂

A COMPLETED TASK

John 17:4

I have glorified thee on earth: I have finished the work which thou gavest me to do. (John 17:4)

There hangs in my office a painting which is a gift, a treasured one from Australian Baptists. The painting was done by Australia's outstanding landscape artist, Sir Hans Heysen. One day during a preaching mission in the lovely and stately city of Adelaide in South Australia, friends drove us out to the country home of Sir Hans to choose a painting. Standing in his studio underneath a skylight in what was once, I am sure, a barn, one could see a number of breathtaking paintings of many parts of the scenic land beneath the Southern Cross. One particular painting caught my eye. It was of the sky toward sunset, presumably, and its colors were bold and eye-arresting. Strangely the painting, so beautiful, in one corner was unfinished. I asked the artist about the canvas. A look of excitement mixed with what I thought was a pensiveness and a wistfulness crossed Sir Hans's face. "I have never been able to finish it," he said with a queer little sadness in the voice. Why? Sir Hans never said, but I assume that the beauty of the sky as the artist saw it had defied and defeated his efforts to capture on canvas what his eyes saw and his heart felt. It was an unfinished task.

Most people are fated to look at the end of their days and see what seems to be an unfinished business, a task not completed. This is one of the saddest aspects about life. We seem so seldom able to complete the job. The symphony of life is almost always an unfinished one. We scarcely come to feel truly secure in our family circles before they are broken, and we have to start all over again getting accustomed to a new circumstance. We hardly

Sermon delivered February 8, 1970.

learn to love those whom God has given us before the day is over and we must part. We only begin to understand the deep and satisfying drama of living before we are called upon to depart from this stage and to go on out into the darkness. Dr. George Buttrick reminds us that a writer's casket bore a copy of his unfinished volume on immortality.

Jesus corrects us about any impression we may have about his own brief, quickly passed life. He says twice as the death angel's wings beat over his pathway that he has done his job, finished his course. In one place, he states his sense of fulfillment in a prayer and lifts before God his short ministry and the deeds he did on the dusty roads of Galilee. He holds it all up with confidence and says, "I have finished the work which thou gavest me to do." What a word! It did not look like it. It seemed that he waited for so long in the carpenter shop at Nazareth and then worked so briefly before they broke him on the grim gallows outside the city's gates.

In nearly thirty years since seminary days at Oberlin I have not forgotten a word which my late roommate, Dr. James Cayce of Ebenezer Church in Pittsburgh, said to me one night during our senior year in the room we shared. "Buddy," he said, "we have spent three years preparing for what may be a ministry of thirty years. Jesus spent thirty years preparing for a ministry of three years." It does seem that he waited so long for his marching orders and then had so short a time to do his work. In the short time he had it looked as if so much went wrong. His life seemed like a beautiful and fragrant flower cruelly and suddenly snapped off. The dreams he had appeared to come to so little. On the very night of our text the Lord Jesus seems to be cornered like an animal. The noose is tightening, the net is closing. Nothing seems to have come out right. The crowds who followed breathlessly once have all gone. The disciples seemed utterly incapable of catching the gleam of glory from his heart. Nobody has seemed to understand. In hours almost he will die, and now he says, "I have finished the work."

There may be some who will say that he did not know then what was waiting for him. Soon they will hurl him unceremoniously upon that cross on Friday and torture him until the body's nerves can bear it no longer and he is dead. Ah, if he had known what was waiting for him he would not be saying so confidently, "I have finished the work which thou gavest me." This is hardly true since a few hours pass and sure enough he is on the cross. He has waded out into the cold rushing river of death. As he nears the other side there is a cry on his lips, "It is finished," and with that shout he passes from mortal sight. So he was claiming completion at the very end. What does it mean?

In his life and in his death Jesus unmasks sin forever for what it is. He finished that task. In my home we have the Mardi Gras, at which time many people mask, far more once than now. You would see the most frightening masks, some of them with ugly gashes and scars, others with wicked leering laughs on their faces. Many a child used to feel an awful terror at seeing the horrible faces of the masks at the Mardi Gras. It was all fun, and people would at the appointed time take off the masks and there behind them were the friendly faces of people whom you knew and among whom you felt secure and at ease. Sin — rebellion against God, human presumption, evil conniving — is exactly the opposite. Sin has always looked like something beautiful. It wears alluring garments and seems so light-hearted. Sin has always deceived men and women because it seems so nice, so harmless, so festive. It appears beautiful and stylish. There is a smile on its face, inviting, welcoming. It seems gentle, so sophisticated, so fashionable. It has ever thus deceived people. Jesus at Calvary snatched the mask from evil and exposed it for what it is.

Evil tried to be tricky with him claiming that it was on the side of the angels, only wanting to protect the people by getting rid of this troublemaker. It would all be done legally and God would be honored, but Jesus outmaneuvered the powers of hell in those events that transpired at his trial and in his death. He would not stand still for the pose, would not accept the mask. When they expected him to say something he kept silent. When they expected silence he spoke. When they lied about him, falsely witnessed against him, screamed at him, whipped him and actually shed his blood, sin showed itself for what it is. It is a liar fooling us. It is a murderer killing us. It is a troublemaker confusing

our family life and dividing us from our friends. It is a fiend tor-
turing us, lashing us. Jesus snatched the mask from the monster
and showed the world that it is hideous and terrible, a crawling,
loathsome thing. He finished the task of showing us the ugliness
of human pride and selfishness, how far it will go, what outrages
it will commit, even against the God presence.

We have seen in greatly diminished proportions the same thing
happen in our country. We in this land have posed as a most civilized and gentle people whose only concerns are law and order.
A good deal of the anger and bitterness abroad in America is due
to the resentment so many feel because events have forced us to
show an ugly racism, a terrifying streak of cruelty, and a sick suspicion about agencies in the life of the nation which should merit
our esteem and respect: the courts, the churches, the schools, the
universities, people of learning and refinement. To compound the
guilt and the anger, there are those in and out of public life who
play upon these fears and suspicions in order to advance their
ambitions and their lust for power. The mask must come off, and
events in our society snatch it off.

This is what Jesus did in his life and his death, showing this
pretender for what it is, and this is what you and I are called
upon to do in our own lives. For we are called upon to walk in
the light as we see the light, and we are called upon once we have
confronted the truth and the truth has confronted us to support
it and serve it. This is the only way our world is going to come
into that bright, particular promise which the Lord who made it
has given to it. He has called us forth to be a part of that purpose. "Every valley shall be filled, and every mountain and hill
shall be brought low, and the crooked shall be made straight, and
the rough places shall be made smooth." To this you and I are
summoned day by day.

ᴄꜱ 25 ᴄꜱ

QUIET COMMUNION AND
NOISY CONFRONTATION

Mark 14:26

And when they had sung an hymn, they went out into the mount of Olives. (Mark 14:26)

Some men sit in soft candlelight whose flicker rises and falls with each gust of wind blowing in from an open window. It is somebody's attic room, doubtless in one of the humbler homes in an undistinguished back street in the great city of David, Jerusalem. One man, obviously the leader of the small and ordinary gathering, is talking with his friends. He talks of vast and mysterious things involving sorrow and death, all related in some strange way to the purposes of God. It is Jesus, and he is keeping the Passover with his disciples. These are men of varied backgrounds and temperaments whom he has selected to be with him.

That upper room must by any judgment be assessed as among the most tender scenes in the Gospels. There is quiet intimacy in that mystic fellowship. One senses the silent sweep of great and tender emotions. These are friends gathered around their faith in God, faith in his promises to Israel, faith in his love for them, faith in the great things that God is about to do. Here in this quiet and reverent scene we behold the gospel in one of its most winsome aspects. We hear the rise and fall of the voice of Jesus as he speaks undying words of parting and comfort. One has only to turn to John's Gospel to catch the tender affection in which the Master holds his friends. A great compassion and concern breaks through the print as he says to them, "Abide in me and I in you." "Peace I leave with you." "My peace I give unto you," and then those infinitely rallying words which have brightened solemn days for

Sermon delivered February 15, 1970.

so many when death has brought a hush and a strange stillness into our homes, "Let not your heart be troubled. In my father's house are many mansions." This is the gospel as we like to think of it. There is quietness and peace, soft lights and rich promises, a steadying hand upon the shoulder, a quiet entreaty spoken in calm terms, a gentle rebuke here and yonder but not with harsh sternness or loudness. There are many who would like to have the blessed gospel of personal reconciliation with God, a private dedication of individual righteousness separated from the broad, burning issues that illumine in awesome light our day and generation.

What we forget is that the quiet and blessed scene to which we have referred was enacted under the immediate threat of cataclysmic and terrifying evils whose approach cast ominous shadows around the gathering. The upper room with its bread and wine was a blessed quietness, but soon there would be strident shouts and angry exclamations by the mob whose torchlights already moved toward a frightening nighttime arrest. The upper room was an hour of mystic fellowship, all charged with the loveliest sentiments and tenderest emotions which human beings have toward God and each other, but soon the ugly glares of hatred and the angry prodding of impatient soldiers' staves and swords would hustle this little company off in the direction of a harsh and prejudicial trial.

Significantly the Scriptures say that when the supper passed and bread had been broken and wine poured in a new act of commemoration, this little band of men, the church in essence, sang a hymn and went out into the Mount of Olives. Ah, there it is in brief compass. They sang a hymn. That symbolizes what we would like our Christian discipleship to be all about. The hymn they sang was a hymn of praise, and we are quite content to let that note fill our worship if it is properly conducted behind appropriate stained-glass windows. Yes, they sang a hymn.

There was more to it than singing a hymn, though without that first part the latter part might well have never been carried off with such gallantry and honor. They sang a hymn and went out into the Mount of Olives. Soon out from the shadows the arresting party would step to do their ugly business. Soon now there would be the sound of arms and the clash of battle. Having sung their hymns these men, following Jesus, went out into an experience filled with sweat and blood and screams and curses and gambling and violence.

We who are Christians are tempted in our pride of respectability to forget that the first Christian community began in such circumstances of violence and ugliness as an illegal society frowned upon by those in authority and hated by the better people. Yes, into all this the disciples went out. When the lovely refrain of the hymn Jesus and his friends sang had died on the evening air, he went out to give to the world a new principle of judgment. His deed at Calvary, the manner of his dying, the triumph he snatched from the surest defeat makes the gospel startlingly relevant to our time and close to our everyday lives. It judges our actions and our loyalties and our confidences in every moment of our lives.

Never after Calvary can people say with any confidence that might makes right. The conquest on that hill and the subsequent capitulation of all Rome's imperial power forever condemn our confidence in the things that can be seen over the things that cannot be seen. Somehow we know looking at him dying and winning that there is a judgment seat set in the midst of our affairs whose decisions determine whether our efforts and hopes stand or fall. Never was a chief of state more right than when the then president of the United States, Lyndon Johnson, whose true greatness waits on recognition, said on an occasion loaded with hope and promise, "Should we defeat every enemy and should we double our wealth and conquer the stars and still be lacking on this issue of human rights, we will have failed as a people and as a nation." For with a country as with a person, what is a man profited if he gains the whole world and loses his own soul?

There is a new principle of judgment thrown against the skyline of the centuries at Calvary. It declares that in this universe steel and legions are not final. In this kind of universe possession of the machinery of state, occupancy of legislatures, control of senates, owning massive industries, and participating in worship in rich and great cathedrals will not guarantee success or mandate survival. This nation with all its wealth and influence will live or die as it meets or fails to meet the purposes of God. Calvary says forever that righteousness exalts a nation, but sin is a reproach to any people.

Having participated in a lovely and gentle act of worship in somebody's upper room and concluding it with a hymn, Jesus and his friends went out to establish a new pattern of humanity. It is one of the ironies of history that the hill called Calvary has become the rallying place of so many hearts in a brave fellowship when it could command the loyalty at first of not a single friend. The chronicle is honest in declaring the craven cowardice and base desertion of almost every member of the disciples' band. My old pulpit idol, the late Paul Scherer, once said in my hearing that as Jesus edged toward his death not a single vote was cast for him. When I suggested that Pilate's wife did cast her vote for Jesus, Dr. Scherer laughed a hearty laugh and replied with characteristic wit, "Yes, but her vote was disqualified." No one stood with him then where now men and women of every kindred and tribe and nation are willing to risk death in the name of his cause, as we have seen so graphically more than once in our land.

The timeless gospel of God's love and human rebellion issuing at Calvary in God's everlasting victory is the basis of a new pattern of fellowship. Ever since the world began people have grouped around some loyalty less than the glory of their Creator and the splendor of their common creaturehood. Always we have assumed that our sense of community must be built upon geography, where we live or of what nation we come. Always we have assumed that our sense of community must be based upon our economics, the amount of our income or the extent of our holdings determining eligibility. Always we have assumed that our community must be established on the basis of externals, color or accent or provincial manners. At Calvary, there has begun a new fellowship. It is not confined to any one race, to any one section of the earth. It is the fellowship of all who have come to believe in the healing of the brokenhearted, in deliverance for the captives, in recovering of sight for the blind, in setting at liberty those that are bruised. This is the new fellowship begun by that cross.

ᵔ 2 6 ᵔ

SEVERAL GLANCES AT THE CROSS

Matthew 27:36

And sitting down they watched him there; . . . (Matthew 27:36)

It was an ugly business, but they were professional soldiers and were not unaccustomed to blood-letting and violence. In the barracks, some of the soldiers must have cursed quietly when they were assigned to the crucifixion of the condemned carpenter, Jesus of Nazareth. It meant a long tour of duty, for every soldier in that part of the world knew that death by crucifixion was more than the utmost in humiliation and shame. It was a slow process, and who could tell how long a man would have to stay out in the heat of day waiting for the end? A man dying on a cross, one old soldier may have told a young legionnaire, died slowly. The mercy of suddenness was denied the person condemned to die by crucifixion. It was this slow torture which made death on the cross a fiendish and ugly method of execution. The condemned was not struck a mortal blow. The was no coup de grace, no finishing or mortal stroke. The body was not broken at any vital point. Only the hands and feet were pierced. Death came by slow exhaustion. The heat of the sun sapped the strength. The foot and hand wounds meant a loss of blood almost drop by drop. Thirst would parch the throat. Heat would scorch the body. Pain would set nerve after nerve raw and quivering. On and on, hour after hour. The soldiers would have to stay on duty, and if the executed was a strong man, well, who knew how long it would be?

With this one, the orders were especially clear and explicit. There were political and religious overtones. The condemned man had a following. Some of them were considered to be rough and dangerous men. The fear on the part of the authorities was that some of the zealots and revolutionaries who had come to

Sermon delivered February 22, 1970.

128

stand under his banner might try to effect a rescue of Jesus in the hope they could staunch the flow of blood and restore him to health. They did not know that his boldest friends had already been routed by fear and in what abject disorder and retreat. The soldiers only knew they were under strict orders to guard this executed carpenter carefully, so "sitting down they watched them there," said one of the writers. What did they see? Some, I am sure, saw nothing but another life snuffed out by public execution. A warning to every one of these crazy colonials not to go too far.

Many of these rude legionnaires gazed for hours on what has touched the world ever since and saw nothing but a dying provincial. They looked on the denouement, the climax, the working out of a purpose hid in God's heart before Adam was born or the morning stars sang together or ever the sons of God shouted for joy, a lamb slain from the foundation of the world — and — saw nothing but another execution. We, too, may look upon that cross without emotion and without faith and hope. Many of us move among the central sanctities of God's dealings with us and are untouched and unimpressed. Prayer, though from the hearts of saints, does not touch us. The hymns of faith and praise leave us cold and indifferent. The preaching of God's Word is boring and tiring. Even the cross, central place of God's redeeming love, the last leap of a determined grace, even the cross towering over the wrecks of time, does not shake us. I have heard men and women uttering within the shadow of that symbol the vilest language which could fall from human lips.

Some of the soldiers sitting down and watching the death of the Son of God saw only some valuable clothes, for one of the few things of earthly value which Jesus possessed was a seamless garment of apparently some expense and worth. The soldiers decided to gamble for that to pass away the time. One man won that garment about which once a poor, haggard, and timid creature at the end of her resources said, "If I can only touch the hem of his garment, I shall be made whole." Sure enough, touching what touched the Lord healed this shy and sick soul. A soldier got it, but minus Jesus, the garment had no power, though an intriguing novel has been written about the robe. There is something tragically pathetic about seeing only something to gain when God is passing by in tragic, regal splendor, about finding nothing more interesting or exciting to do than to gamble for such low stakes when Christ is betting his very life on God and on us. Sitting down, they watched him there.

What could one see glancing up at that cross and then perhaps looking away and then glancing at it again? Well, those soldiers might have seen, and we might see, in the death of Jesus our cravenness, our unwillingness to stand no matter the odds for what is right. Christ did not just die. He died because people did not have the courage to resist evil in themselves. Did not have the spiritual resources to stand up for truth. Pilate, who tried to wash his hands, was weak, for in the issues of life, in the real issues of life, we are called upon to choose sides, not to slink away from difficulty. The easiest thing in the world, most of the time, is to quit. I say most of the time because, admittedly, it is sometimes the hardest thing in the world to do. Moral weariness, tiredness with the good fight overtakes us all. We grow weak and irresolute. It is at that moment that our guard is down and the cause of right and truth can be set back. These soldiers looking at what that cross represented might have seen the fickleness of the crowd, their willingness to be manipulated and handled. The way they ran wildly from any hard thinking, their herd-mindedness — that put the Son of God on Calvary. Next, when you fail to face up to an issue, lie to yourself, or sneak away from an honorable path because it is difficult, just remember that in so doing, you help to crucify the Son of God afresh.

Another glance — perceptive and open-spirited — would have shown those men who watched, the spectacle of wickedness at its worst. There are times when evil which is always with us concentrates its terrible and awesome power. At some point in history for a major engagement, it throws in incalculable forces of resourceful and wicked might. I believe such moments can be identified now and again. Mad Nero burning Rome and murdering Christians by the thousands was an occasion of evil's concentrated, mass assault on all that is decent and right. The unspeakable cruelty of human slavery was such a time. The Hitler insanity in which six million people died was a moment of evil's intense and awesome, focused power. The cross on Calvary represents evil at its worst. There the most sinister coalition of sheer evil met and massed and marched against the powers of God. Calvary was nothing less than hell's key attack, its long conceived and plotted assault upon the throne place of the universe, upon God.

Another glance at the cross would have shown God in Christ at his grandest, engaged in the greatest demonstration of love of which his heart could conceive. No wonder John Calvin wrote, "There is no tribunal so magnificent, no throne so stately, no show of triumph so distinguished, no chalice so elevated as the gibbet, the gallows on which Christ has subdued death and the devil and trodden them under his feet." At Calvary, Jesus showed us how much God will suffer for us and to what lengths he will go in our behalf. Midst curses, he prayed. Midst jeers, he talked with God. Midst failure, he traveled in the greatness of his strength. Dying, he saved the dying; he beat back the death angel's wings and saw a thief clear across the dark rolling tide; at Calvary he led captivity captive. So the Bible says in its soaring imagery. On Calvary's hill, Christ unmasked evil's pretensions once and for all, snatched the offensive from the forces of Satan, arrested the drift of history, and rechanneled the centuries toward God. We may not understand all that this century-splitting act of crucifixion means, but we know in some deep and indescribable way that it was for us. And now, because of it, we stand in a new and glorious inheritance.

❧ 27 ❧

THREE CROSSES ON A HILL

Luke 23:32–33

And there were also two other, malefactors, led with him to be put to death. And when they were come to the place, which is called Calvary, there they crucified him, and the malefactors, one on the right hand, and the other on the left. (Luke 23:32–33)

There were three crosses on that hill. Joseph Sittler, the eminent Lutheran theologian, said that a cross is not a pretty symbol. A circle has about it a satisfying sense of completeness. It meets itself. A curve has a certain grace. It arcs gradually and, therefore, does not assault the senses as being ugly or jarring. On the other hand, a cross does not proceed in any one direction. It starts upward in the vertical beam, on which the condemned is placed, as if to say "yes" to something, justice or whatever you wish. The cross piece, upon which the arms are outstretched, seems to contradict the upward beam, saying "no." It is a symbol of brokenness and opposites. By God's grace and his amazing strategy, the perfect completion of the circle is not the master sign of God's care and God's triumph, nor is the symmetry, the beauty of a curve, the sign place of our redemption. But rather an ugly, rude, crude, cruel cross is God's mark of our deliverance and restoration to his good favor. Neither the debasement of bigots nor questions about the quality of the music can impair the love millions have for that hymn which has in it the words "On a hill far away stood an old rugged cross, the emblem of suffering and shame. And I love that old cross, where the dearest and best for a world of lost sinners was slain."

Indeed, there were three crosses on a bleak and rocky hill that fateful Friday, when God threw into our fight all that he had. Three crosses. Two of them told the old, old story that the

Sermon delivered March 1, 1970.

wages of sin is death. Two of those crosses on Calvary's brow that Friday were cases of "chickens coming home to roost," for on two of these crosses were two thieves, criminals. They lived by violence and might, and therefore they died by violence and naked might. They were evidence that there is a place real and sure where malefactors are punished. No man can run counter to God's will and men's highest insights of justice without running out. Two of those crosses told a grim story of men getting what they gave and underscored the old word that "bread cast upon the water will in not many days return unto its sender increased many fold." They got what was coming to them.

One has only to consider the history of our country to see that what is wrong may persist, but it cannot win. The cause of human freedom has seemed so helpless so often in this republic. Its opponents so mighty and with such interlocking advantages of wealth and communication and influence. Yet, with all the nation's shortcomings, who can contradict that the enemies of human freedom, changing as they have from place to place and from one group to another, have never been able, really, to trample and stifle the claims which our nation has staked out as its purpose in history? Look again at people whose aims have been low and whose power has seemed so great. They prance for a moment in their strength, their names spoken in fear or envy by every lip. They seem beyond any laws of humanity or God. But look again, first at this one and then at that one, and see how they come toppling from their pedestals. There seems to be a kind of law, doesn't there? Ah, will you with me call him God?

There was a third cross, the cross of Jesus. He died just like the others. What's the payoff for being good? He died, too. Admit it. Yes, he died, too, because all men die. High religion does not cloak the truth that the righteous are likely to suffer because they are righteous. Human beings hate what they are superior to, and they hate what they are inferior to. They will crucify on the same hill those who are less than they are and those who are more than they are. The cross of Jesus says also that "without the shedding of blood, there is no remission of sins." Somebody must pay a price every time a new and creative miracle takes place. Every generation must die improving the opportunities of the next. Every mother must nearly die to bring a new life into the world. Morning comes by way of the nighttime. Spring arrives through the cold path of winter. The rainbow arcs only after a stormy sky. Flowers must come up out of dirt. So the third cross. It was redemptive, purposeful, a dark cloud out of which there glowed the glory of a rainbow spanning the threatening heavens.

Let us look again at the cross on the left. A hard man writhes on it in agony. But no whimper crosses his lips to give satisfaction to his tormentors. He has lived by the sword, and he is dying by it. He is still cursing his executioners as he stands on the threshold of death. I am calling his case that of stubborn resentment. Now, there is a certain admiration we have for the man who will not break under hard and trying conditions. A popular poll some years ago revealed that Humphrey Bogart was the chief idol of the men at one of our greatest universities because in his movies he laughed in the face of fear and dared death while holding nothing too dear. We can admire that in the cross on the left. But when a soul faces the holy, it ought to be hushed and humbled.

There is something terrifying about a man laughing in God's face or taunting and mocking sacrifice and love. We would recoil at a man rejoicing when his mother is in pain or dancing while his child dies or cursing someone who is helping him out of a hard place. Far worse it is to stand in the presence of the holy with nothing in the heart and on the lips but a sneer. There are some places where the voice ought to be hushed and where we ought to tiptoe. That first cross shows a hardhearted man with nothing but a taunt and a sneer on his lips as he watches the Son of God working out in letters of blood the word of our redemption. Listen to him: "If thou be the Son of God, come down from thy cross and save us and thyself."

There was on Jesus' right another cross. It was not a good man on it. He had not done anything, this thief on the right, to earn anybody's sympathy or respect. But there is one thing to be said in his favor. When he saw truth in Jesus, he had the sense and the grace to recognize it. He had in his business seen many men die, doubtless, but this was different. This was no victim he saw, slowly sinking into the defeat of death. This was a king, regal in bearing, marching, not staggering through a blood-soaked valley to his coronation. This was no ordinary sufferer. This, saw the thief, was a savior carrying in his strong arms the helpless beneficiaries of his grace, lifting them up steep steps of sorrow toward God's throne. This poor thief had nothing to offer, could only cry, so to speak, "Nothing in my hand I bring, only to thy cross I cling." He reached out an empty hand, but a sincere and pleading one. "Lord, I can see you are en route to receive a crown. When the river is crossed and the hill is climbed and the gates swing wide, Lord, when thou comest into thy kingdom, remember me." That prayer opened the gates of a new life to a dying man. Jesus snatched him out of the abyss and void, put his arm around him, and carried him on home to God.

There was, of course, the third cross. The middle one. The center of the gaze of the centuries. The subject of the loftiest poetry and the theme of innumerable musicians. It was the cross of Jesus. The Scriptures are lean and terse in their description of it. I dare not dwell upon the physical pain of that awful hill. Far, far deeper was the spiritual agony and desolation through which the Savior passed to bring our wandering souls home to God. His was a voluntary death, for the sins and wrongs of others, and in which he had no guilt. All others who have died in some way were part of the evil on which they turned. But not Jesus. Name the other martyrs. Socrates drinking his hemlock was a part of the Athens he condemned and for which condemnation he died. Abraham Lincoln was a part of this nation and profited in some sense from the slavery which he attacked and, in attacking, died. Name any of them, and they were a part of what they hated and what killed them. Not Jesus. The worst they could say was that he stirred up the crowd. Some said he went about doing good, and yet sinless, he died for sin. Spotless, he took upon himself our spots. Countless millions have found that in what he did their lives have been infinitely enriched and enlarged. Thinking of what he has done ought to make you hold your head a little higher in dignity and offer your heart a little more willingly in service to all for whom he cared so much.

ᨓ 2 8 ᨓ

Only Scarred Hands Heal

Revelation 5:9

And they sung a new song, saying, Thou art worthy to take the book, and to open the seals thereof: for thou wast slain, and hast redeemed us to God by thy blood out of every kindred, and tongue, and people, and nation; ... (Revelation 5:9)

Thornton Wilder has a one-act play entitled "The Angel that Troubled the Waters." He depicts the scene at the pool of Bethesda where a great multitude of people wait for the propitious moment when the angel comes down and endows the pool with spiritual power which turns the stream into healing waters. Among the anxious cripples is one who times without number has come to the pool in the hope that on that particular day his own infirmities might be healed and his horribly twisted and deformed body might be straightened out. Others have always rushed in in front of him, and he has had to turn back, still misshapen and grotesquely crippled. On this particular day, he appeals in desperation to the angel to help him into the water so that he might be healed and made whole. His appeal is brushed aside as the angel whispers to him, "Stand back, healing is not for you. Without your wound where would your power be? It is your very remorse that makes your low voice tremble into the hearts of men. Not the angels themselves in heaven can persuade the wretched blundering children of earth as can one human being broken on the wheels of living. In love's service only wounded soldiers can serve."

The book of Revelation strikes this note like the diapason swell of a great organ in the fifth chapter. The scene is a mysterious and cryptic one. Like most of the book, this chapter is wrapped in strange and solemn figures and symbols. The chapter talks about

---

Sermon delivered March 8, 1970.

a book sealed with seven seals. We are not told what the book means nor its significance for us and our salvation. The writer is a spectator in this solemn drama of divine mystery. He says he sees a strong angel who cries in a loud voice, "Who is worthy to open the book and to loose the seals?" Apparently the angel flies through the heavens like a celestial courier sounding the query across the vast places of eternity. Who is worthy? Angels seem to lower their gaze and to bow their heads, for nowhere in all that vastness is there found one with the strength of spirit to open the crucial book. There is something about the opening of the book which makes it the key to the conquering of Satan and necessary to the deliverance of humanity from the captivity of sin itself. Then the earth was examined for someone who could reveal the words of the book, but to no avail. Following this, a search was instituted beneath the earth, but here again the survey was in vain and the searcher admitted failure. At about this time the writer said that he could bear it no longer. "I wept much," he said, "because no one was found worthy to open and to read the book."

At this juncture in the strange pageant, one of the heavenly figures says, "Weep not. Behold the lion of the tribe of Judah, the root of David, hath prevailed to open the book. And, lo, in the midst of the throne stood a lamb as it had been slain." He strode to the throne and took the book. At this point in the mystic drama there breaks through the heavenly places a song never heard before in the eternities. "Thou art worthy to take the book and to open the seals because thou wast slain." So the power was because of the scars.

We all draw back from the sting of trouble and from the pain of being wounded. It is natural for us to want to avoid pain and discomfort. Only the morbidly diseased person courts hurt and enjoys being wounded. So many of us are obsessive on the other side. We intend to avoid pain and trouble at any price. "I do not want to get hurt" is the theme of so many of us. We go through life trying to avoid all situations that might involve damaged emotions and bruised feelings. So we go sliding through the days, but this is not living. True living consists of believing

greatly, not narrowly, parochially, coyly. True living consists of
risking grandly, not pettily and miserly. True living consists of loving deeply, not cautiously, carefully. True living consists of daring
nobly, not hedging every action. Donald Hankey said that this is
the essence of great religion. "I bet my life there is a God," he
said. Here is a gambler with stakes worthy of an immortal soul.
To love truly, to care greatly, to believe deeply, to dare nobly will
likely get you some wounds, but wait, you and I will never come
to the stature God intended us to have unless we do get some
scars. There is something in you so worthful that it makes you
the most precious commodity in the universe. To get that something released and set in use, some wounding must take place. "In
love's service only wounded soldiers can serve."

If you have been hurt by betrayal or wounded by desertion or
scarred by defeat or reverses, the first thing you ought to do is to
say to God, "I do not know why I have this trouble in my life,
but I believe you, Father, can get more glory out of my life since
the scar has come. And so here and now I offer to you, God, my
wounded heart. It is a broken spirit that I am giving, not shiny
and new, but cut up and in pieces. Take it, if you can use it."
When this happens, an incalculable endowment is bestowed on
the one who so offers. The scar becomes a center of power. Nor is
it so hard to explain. Who would you rather hear and heed, someone who said to you, "Well, I don't have any notion what you are
going through, but I would like to help"? Or someone who said,
"I have sat where you sit. I have been in the place where you are
now, and I want to help you"? Such scarred hands heal. I think
it is for that reason that older people who are good people have
so much inner strength to give their juniors. They have weath-
ered many a storm, and the strains and stresses have made them
strong like oaks. They have borne burdens in the heat of the day,
and their burden bearing has given them an inner capacity for
sympathy and encouragement.

The account in Revelation suggests that even God's Son to get
to saviorhood had to travel the way of sorrow and betrayal and
loneliness and pain. No poet, never mind how sweet his meter,
was found worthy to break the seals. No soldier, no matter how

victorious his campaigns, was found worthy to break the seals. No statesman, no matter how astute his diplomacy, was found worthy to break the seals. Then one with thorn marks in his brow and with a heart broken by a friend's betrayal and with his spirit wounded by many false charges stepped forward. The one who is able to open the book upon which our deliverance depended had hands marked by nail prints. The scars gave power, and therefore the great anthem was heard ringing across the celestial plains, "Worthy is the lamb that was slain to receive power and riches and strength and honor and glory and blessing." "Thou art worthy to take the book and to open the seals, for thou wast slain." The marks of power were in the scars.

I would like a life like that. Wouldn't you? Few of us will have great political power or enormous economic resources. Each of us can have a spiritual power to make people feel a little better and dare a little more nobly wherever we walk. What more could you ask than to be able to cheer the weary traveler, to throw a little sunshine in somebody's bleak midnight? There are people like that, you know. They got that way, received that power because they were willing to risk hurt in high service, were willing that the pretty petals be crushed in order that a rare fragrance of the spirit might belong to them. There is really no other way that this can take place, except by one being willing to expose himself or herself to "the slings and arrows of outrageous fortune" in a good cause. Do you know how my own forebears talked about such hurts? They sang "Gonna shoulder up my cross. Gonna take it home to Jesus. Ain't a that good news?" Yes, this is good news, very good news. For along this way of life there are many people who are deeply hurt, and when they are met by one who has also been hurt and who out of that hurt is ready to help, great healing occurs.

⌒ 29 ⌒

THE COMING OF THE GREAT KING

Luke 19:41–44

And when he was come near, he beheld the city, and wept over it, . . . (Luke 19:41)

The holiday crowds were gathering in the city of Jerusalem from everywhere. It was close to Passover time. Ships were completely booked from all Mediterranean ports. There were caravans with innumerable swaying camels and foot travelers by the hundreds. By every mode of travel, pilgrims were coming to Jerusalem for its highest of holy days. The city itself high on Mt. Zion had taken on a gay and festive air. Hucksters loudly announced their wares in the bazaars along the narrow passage of King David Street and other thoroughfares. Friends bumped into each other and traded the gossip of their villages. Hotels and inns were crammed to the rafters. Fortunate were they who had kindred in Jerusalem, for such people could claim the hospitality of a brother's or cousin's roof. The city was heavy with expectancy. A wistful hope filled the air with anxious waiting for the coming of Messiah, the deliverance of God. The prophets had been studied and restudied for hints of when God would fling the thunderbolt of his judgment against the arrogant Roman authority whose swaggering overlordship drew muttered curses from the clenched teeth of every Israelite who looked at the passing soldiers from eyes that burned with the fires of hatred. Prophets had promised that God would deliver.

Isaiah had said a king would reign in righteousness, God's King. This same poet had declared that their eyes would see the king in his beauty. When he would come the eyes of all would see, and under his blessed reign Jerusalem would be "a quiet habitation, a tabernacle that shall not be taken down. Not one

---

Sermon delivered March 29, 1970.

of the stakes thereof shall ever be removed, neither shall any of the cords thereof be broken." This heavenly king, Isaiah had declared, would be unto his people like "a place of broad rivers and streams. The LORD is our King; he will save us."

Such was the hope on that holy day. Friend asked friend in the streets of the city, "Do you think God will do it now? Do you? Is this the year?" The Gospel of Luke states that a king was indeed on his way to Jerusalem. This is how that writer put it: "And when he was come near, he beheld the city and wept over it." Such was the arrival of Jesus on what we have come to call Palm Sunday. The entry was God's presentation of himself in his kind of kingship to the city of the great King. Jerusalem was the natural setting for this coronation. More steeped in the ways of God than Athens in her heathen thought or Rome in her pagan power, Jerusalem was the natural place for God to offer his love and leadership, his grace and guidance to the children of the prophets. Their fathers had heard the thunders at Sinai. One of their forebears had wrestled with God at Jabbok Brook. Their ancestor David had slain Goliath in the plains of Israel. To whom else would God offer his kingship than to a people who had been blessed with such dealings as they had had with him? The lyrics of Isaiah had moved through their history, the stern forebodings of Jeremiah were their heritage, the bold condemnation of Amos flamed in the national memory. To whom else would God turn as King save to those who had the most and best chance to know him? Who else would be in such position to receive him? Yes, and who else would be so anxious to surrender lives and hopes, fortune and future to the tender dominion of his rulership? It was natural for God to come unto his own. Deep would be calling unto deep.

In experience of the holy, we and citizens of old Jerusalem are indeed one. God offers his kingship to all of us who have from the earliest moments of our lives been privileged to see and sense his goodness. God offers his rule to our lives because we have had experience of him and of his goodness. He comes offering his kingship only to those who have had knowledge of him, who ought to be anxious, eager, trembling to have him reign.

The procession moves closer even as he bears down on your heart and mine right now. He beholds the city and its people as he draws nearer. Jesus of Nazareth is arriving at Jerusalem and seeing the City of David at close hand. There seems to be a hesitancy and a halt in the procession as he looks at the city of the great King. There is a view of the buildings on Mt. Zion. The blazing bronze doors of the temple stood on the eastern heights of the city. The temple's shining dome blazed in the brilliance of the morning sunlight. Across the Kedron Valley, a frowning fortress looked down from the north. He could see the palace of Herod with its three famous towers dominating the western front of the city. Around the extremities of the town the eyes of Jesus must have caught sight of the old wall, stained by years of heat and dust, breached on all sides by gates, one of them the Damascus out of which not a century later a little Jew named Paul would march to change the face of the world. On the northeastern side the fish gate, on the western side the gate of David. As he beheld the city he could see the pool of Siloam nestling in a valley of the metropolis.

Jesus saw the city of Jerusalem, but he saw more. A people called his name, but their loyalties were far from him. They went through the motions of religion, but they lacked the power of real affection for God. They sang the psalm anthems, but there was no solemn commitment in their hearts. They raised their altars, but no real fires of faith leapt toward the skies. They were religionists without being religious, performers but not participants. They talked ethics but did not practice the presence of God. They knew the law but refused to obey the promptings of the soul. He beheld the city and saw corruption in high places. He beheld the city and saw hatred and meanness gathering around the altar of God. Materialists talked about spirituality but lived under the slavery of Mammon. He beheld the city, but saw more.

Now the King draws near to you and to me, to us who ought to thrill to his presence, who ought to respond with every quivering nerve to his grace. He beholds you and me. Underneath our mask of pious goodness the Lord Christ knows that we reject him. We live by our wits instead of by our faith in him. We live by scheming instead of by his power, by our dislikes rather than by his love. Told to be quietly confident because he loves us, we are rather anxious and fretted. Told to put our affection on things above, we live rather by our lust below. Told that we are a colony of heaven, we have taken citizenship in the city of Mammon.

He beheld a city and as the procession stops a minute, a sad and pained frown crosses his calm countenance. He seems to look around, and his spirit trembles as if hearing the growing thunder of approaching judgment. The eyes of Jesus dim with tears. He wept! This is Christ weeping in love at the sins of his people who seem to accept him but whose hearts are far from him. He weeps! This is God's sorrow, the heartbreak of the eternal. Ought not this to melt our hearts? The grand, solemn, tragic procession moves on past where you and I stand and on to Calvary. As he passes now in still another offering of himself, you and I ought to fling ourselves recklessly and magnificently in the path behind him. A word half shouted, half whispered up out of our inmost selves ought to be our declaration of intention.

> Lead on, O King Eternal,
> The day of march has come;
> Henceforth in fields of conquest
> Thy tents shall be our home.
> Through days of preparation
> Thy grace has made us strong,
> And now, O King Eternal,
> We lift our battle song.

∽ 3 0 ∾

Still Another Look at Calvary

Luke 23:33

And when they were come to the place, which is called Calvary, there they crucified him, . . . (Luke 23:33)

Do you not find it strange that the world cannot get over Calvary and the crucifixion of Jesus of Nazareth? There were other events in the life of Jesus, the tense and mighty drama of temptation, the calling of the Twelve, the healing miracles, the Sermon on the Mount, the parables. Yes, we talk about them, but Calvary, the crucifixion, has a special place in our hearts and thoughts so much so that we hesitate to deal publicly with that event's effect upon us. Charles Spurgeon, in his generation, advised young preachers that no matter where they started in their sermons, they should make their way as rapidly as possible across country to Calvary. There is something about Jesus' crucifixion which excites deep considerations and which says something final about the love of God and which gives us a bright and blessed hope. The spirituals of my own people have many haunting moods and tunes that touch the heart, but I know of none that leaves us so defenseless utterly as that one about the crucifixion: "Were you there when they crucified my Lord? Oh, sometimes it causes me to tremble, tremble, tremble."

This hill outside of Jerusalem with the innocent God-man dying on it is a gospel, a good news, if you please, sufficient to take the breath away. There was a play off Broadway some seasons back in which a point was reached where the audience was invited to ask questions which the leading character would answer. On the night I saw the play one of the questions from the audience was about Christianity and revolution. The incredibly ignorant and sneering reply of the leading character was "There

Sermon delivered March 22, 1970.

is your Christian God out there somewhere in thin air and not even strong enough to be a man." In this the actor missed, as so many people do, the very central word of the New Testament, the essence, the core, the heart of the gospel.

The Christian gospel is all about a God who loved enough, was strong enough, brave enough, who cared enough to become a man, the man Christ Jesus, the second Adam, a new start for humanity, the first of many brethren. The Christian gospel specifies that in Christ God has not only become man in order to get with us but also has entered the deepest and most convulsive experiences of which the human soul is capable. This gospel speaks of no distant abstraction, no majestic injunction uttered from some remote and invisible mount. This gospel is of a birth and a childhood and a manhood of tears and laughter, of friendships and feasts, of loneliness and sorrow, of death, the stuff of our own life into which God has come. We have a God who was strong enough to become a man like those whom he loved that they might become like him whom they were born to love.

The supreme moment of victory in the life of Christ among us occurred at Calvary. The Gospel writers would not, could not elaborate and rhapsodize upon the event. You read all four of the accounts of the crucifixion as they appear in Matthew, in Mark, in Luke, in John, and in none of them will you see any flabby phrases, any ponderous passages, any purple and florid oratory. Each Gospel writer who recorded the supreme act of God's love, the last fatal plunge of God's care, the final thrust of God's mercy, gives the Calvary account with terse leanness. "When they were come to the place called Calvary, there they crucified him."

Take another look at Calvary and you will see there the ugly, stubborn mystery of sin. We tend to see this rebellion against God, this repudiation of love, this turning of oneself inward, this separation from others, from God and from our true selves, this willfulness, this self-centeredness, this shutting out of goodness and grace, this sinfulness as something annoying, maybe, but not really bad. We are likely to wink at wrong and to laugh it off or call it smart. A man all for himself we do not call a sinner. He is "go-getter" and "a sharp dealer," we say with a tinge of admiration. A drunkard is not one who is living life shamefully below his high and sacred potential but "a good-timer," "a swinger." Self-centered women we are likely to call stylish and sophisticated. People who betray public trust and are discovered merely outsmarted themselves in what everybody does. People who spread the poison of hatred for other human beings may be widely honored by government or church; thus we make sin attractive, dashing, gay, splendid, admirable. It is well-groomed and sort of enviable. Calvary exposes the hideous quality of human sin. Sin, men of moral laxity and ambition and pride and religious snobbery and cowardice and self-interest, put Jesus on his cross. Sin, the kind of cheap compromising with principle which you and I practice, put the sword in his side.

There is something in us humans that is cruel and wicked and not to be smiled at and which needs to be plucked out before it spoils all of life and stains all around us with shame and disgrace. We need to recognize this. We need God's grace to cleanse us, to deliver us from presumptuousness, to free us from the captivity of our own fleshly desires and impulses, to emancipate us from the death-dealing envy and prejudice which reside in all of us. Sin, self-centeredness of class, section, race can destroy our land, and so Jesus at Calvary made sin, human evil, overstretch, expose itself for what it really is. People looking at sin lying, screaming, plotting the death and crucifying the Son of God must forever cry, "This is hideous, ugly, repulsive."

Still another look at Calvary shows us the mystery of triumphant assurance. Someone has spoken of a monument somewhere in Europe, I think, where it was said of the man whose likeness was on the monument that he "did the best of things in the worst of times." Doubtless an excessive compliment of any one human, but this can surely be said of Jesus. In the midst of all that flood of hatred, those rolling tides of anger and poisoned determination, no word of vengeance ever falls from the lips of the Son of God. He did not consider himself powerless, for had he not said in the garden that there stood at his beck and call a vast and incalculable spiritual reinforcement? Remember his words, "Thinkest thou that I cannot now pray to my Father, and he shall presently give me more than twelve legions of angels?" Yet while mad men rage around him and pain makes every nerve a raw and quivering agony, no word of resentment falls from his lips. Instead one hears a strange prayer for his tormentors. "Father, forgive them, for they know not what they do." When I hear him pray that prayer, I know this is no ordinary man. When I hear him pray this prayer, I know I am in the presence of a great Savior.

Those who stood around and jeered him unconsciously paid to him a high and holy compliment. They said, to mock him, "He saved others. Let him save himself." He did save others because he would not save himself. Those scorners missed the point. Any man who would really help others cannot help himself. An older sister giving up her life for the younger children left without parents cannot save for herself the ordinary joys of marriage and home. The father of modest means seeking to save his child from ignorance cannot save himself with clothes and comforts. The Christian seeking to win others to a new life cannot save himself from unfriendly response and uncertainty as to how his word about Christ will be received. We know Jesus is truly the Lord precisely when he saves others and cannot save himself.

Now these last brief words. I cannot explain it all. Standing there at Calvary, musing upon it, bowing the head and opening the heart, we know something has been done for us that nobody but Jesus could do. We reach for figures and metaphors. There the old account is settled. There the separating veil is torn in two. There the prisoner's cell door swings wide. There is something about that lonely, lightless hill called Calvary which delivers us.

℘ 31 ℘

A Strange Question in a Cemetery

John 20:15

Jesus saith unto her, Woman, why weepest thou? (John 20:15)

A hope is in people's hearts today. It is Easter! The perennial faith blossoms again. The wistful dream of life being stronger than death returns with the certainty of springtime. It is Easter, and the mighty anthems of hope are loosed in the human heart. The grand "perhaps," the great "maybe" that this is not all comes back in vigor and force. It is Easter! The dark forebodings lift. The dark depths of the grave bear a beam of light. How we need Easter; without it life is petty and tragic, what with darkness and cold off at the end of the little day we are given.

I stood not too long ago with a man in a hospital room. His eyes were sunken circles of sorrow and heartbreak. The sob in his soul shook his whole body. His voice quavered and broke, and there was about it an immense sadness. In the bed lay a lean and tossing frame. It was his wife, and she was valiantly but painfully fighting for breath. The specter of death hovered over the room. I asked the man finally, "How long have you two been married?" He looked at me, and a heartrending sorrow was in his face and in his words when he answered, "Forty-seven years, and now I can't do anything for her." Is that what life is all about? Is it a bright day doomed to an everlasting night when the lights will go out and there will be nothing left forever? See that family all laughing and gay, with little children playing happily around their mother and father. What a sight of joy and peace! But one day a dark cloud will settle over that happy family. Laughter will be silenced, and smiles will be frozen. Death will enter, and there will be one less of that happy circle and then another. For our

---

Sermon delivered April 5, 1970.

dearest loves are doomed to wither at the hand of cruel time. Is this all for which we can hope? Is it any wonder that Paul cried out, "If in this life only we have hope in Christ we are of all men most miserable"? The happiest life, joined as it is to death, has over it a shadow.

Wrong seems forever on the throne, truth forever on the scaffold. Evil flexes mighty muscles and takes away the peace and joy of life. We seem never to escape from warfare with the powers of darkness. There are lies and deceit and injustice and violence and schemes and ugly maneuvers. Sin is in the land casting its withering blight on the sons of men. We see it in our nation, turning a people who are trustees of history's highest undertaking into a snarling, screaming, screeching society of suspicion and conflict. Is this our fate, to know nothing better than a grim and losing battle against the powers of sin and the sting of death? And at last to go down to a lonely grave, broken, defeated?

That was the way it looked with the people who loved the Lord and who followed him to the end. His death on that fearful Friday meant that evil thinking, as men, evil walking, as men, evil talking, as men, had done him in. They had killed the prince of glory. What had he done? His judge said he found no fault in him. Those who knew him most intimately said he went about doing good. When they nailed him to the cross, some sarcastically screamed, "He trusted in God. Let God deliver him now if he will have him." Now he was dead. The bright burnished dream had ended as a horrible, bloody nightmare. The high holy crusade had ground to a stop in an ignominious ditch. The splendid hope was now a mangled despair. Hands that had healed the sick bore now the ugly scar of a cruel spike. Hands that had touched the blind, healed the sick, and cleansed the leper were now frozen in the chill clutch of death. Those shining eyes, full of grace and truth which had stilled the tempest in human souls and inspired frightened people to be brave, were now fixed in the stare of death. That voice which had sounded like the singing of angels was silenced in the stillness of the grave. They had taken him down and buried him in Joseph's new tomb. The high adventure which had started in a cradle in Bethlehem had ended on a cross on

Calvary, and Jesus was now a bruised and broken corpse in a cemetery.

Still, love is a stubborn thing. It somehow goes on anyhow. Love is perhaps the most persistent thing on earth. It marches on through disaster and disappointment. Love shoulders up its load and keeps on climbing, though the ascent is steep and dizzying. Though there are barriers and blockades, it never stops marching. I do not say now what I am going to say in any flippant or critical sense but in admiration for the believing stubborn quality of love. I have never, or rarely ever, seen a mother coming to talk to me about her child's problems in school or with the courts who did not in some way qualify the child's wrong or minimize it or make some sort of excuse for it. This is a mother's love and reveals itself a stubborn, determined thing. Women and men have gone on twenty and thirty years in the hope that they could change the failings of their marriage partners. For love has a persisting stubborn quality. It goes on.

Early on Sunday morning after the crucifixion, Mary, whose sins had been forgiven, got up early to go where they had laid him. She could not do much. He was dead and discredited, but she loved her Lord and simply wanted to be there. A cemetery is so final and hopeless, but Mary could not stay away. Love woke her up, pushed her out of her home, and drove her to the cemetery. Love will go to a cemetery and beyond. If you do not believe it, go into almost any cemetery at Easter or All Saints Day and you will see people standing humbly and wistfully around little mounds of earth with their love offerings of flowers and plants. You will see that love is a stubborn, determined thing. Not even death can stop it. Dr. George Buttrick reported that a woman once said, "Twenty years ago my child died. If he had lived he would be twenty-four today." Twenty years and love had not forgotten, but love is at last only a sad, defeated, desolate, quality if death is final.

Mary's love of her Lord posted her there in the hopelessness of the cemetery. That same stubborn, touching love put tears of great sorrow in her eyes and an immeasurable sadness in her heart. She had come to that human border where there was nothing to do but weep, and then came the strange question, so very strange to be asked in a cemetery, "Woman, why weepest thou?" Why ask such a question in a cemetery? A cemetery is a place for crying, for it writes *finis* over our love affairs. It is the scene of our earthly separations. A cemetery is a silent place where friends speak back to us no longer. It is a cold place where love's springtime is chilled in an unmelting winter. Why ask anybody, "Why do you cry" when that person is in a cemetery? What else is there to do? An inept, cruel question, unless it is Jesus speaking.

Faith declares that question to be not so strange on the first Easter morning, for Jesus was there in the cemetery and alive and said to her, "Mary," and his voice rang joyously in the saddened depths of her soul. It made a difference. Jesus was there and alive, and this made that cemetery so very different. It still does. I am sure we will go on weeping when we lose our loved ones, but we shall weep now as those who have hope. Jesus has been here now, and we can raise up our bowed-down heads. Jesus has been here now, and we can believe that while we may be separated we shall meet again where the load has lifted and the gate opens wide. Jesus has been here now, and we can believe that "life is ever lord of death, and love can never lose its own." Jesus has been here now, and we can believe that somewhere there is a land beyond the river, a land whose fields are living green. Then let the glad anthems of Easter ring, for Jesus has been here.

❧ 32 ❧

A Word to Young Preachers on the Name of the Savior

John 1:1–17

Our Father and our God, we thank thee for the bright beauty of early morning and for the swift and awful gift of life, for its opportunities and obligations, for its light moments and for its solemn times. We thank thee for every gift which gives grace and gladness to our days. Family, friends, the privilege of responsibility and, above all, for that unspeakable and amazing gift, Jesus Christ, our Lord. How empty, our Father, and barren would our lives be had he not been here. We thank thee for the joy and the hope and for the solemn obligations which come to us because of him. We recognize that we are not worthy to be called thy children, and yet thou, through him, hast given us that great and rich privilege. Grant that we may ever be mindful of our unworthiness and ever seek to become worthy, always recognizing that we are saved by thy grace and thy mercy. We thank thee, our Father, for the church, for all of its long and grand history, for the saints who from their labors rest, and for all who have helped to make it a community of faith and love. We thank thee that we have grown up in its midst, that we have been nurtured upon its gospel, that we have found in it inspiration and light and love. Grant, our Father, that in this our day and generation we may give a good account of ourselves as members of the household of faith.

We pray, our Father, for all who have gathered here, for the young who are coming now into the full use of their powers and for those in the middle years who carry the responsibilities of life, and we pray for any who have come now to the setting of the sun. Grant that as life's little day fades there may come upon them, ever brighter, that morning which shall know no evening. Bless us now in the proclamation of the Word of God, and give to all

---

These musings were delivered as part of a lecture series at Union Theological Seminary in Richmond, Virginia, on February 1, 1978, and are not part of the NBC radio series. They are included in this first volume because of the relevance of the message. They are my gift to those who set out to preach the gospel of Jesus Christ. —*GCT*

of these who have gathered here a good day and a good work and at evening something which all of us might hold up before thee and feel not too ashamed. May thy blessings be upon us now, in our going out and in our coming in, in our rising up and in our sitting down, in our laughter and in our tears, in our joy and in our sorrow until that day which is without dawn and without dusk; through Jesus Christ our Lord. Amen.

I suppose that from time to time we all wonder about how empowered we are or are going to be to proclaim the Word of God. I have found great encouragement in an incident which happened in the earlier years of Charles Haddon Spurgeon. Already his reputation had begun to spread, and he had gone back to Kelveden to preach in that neighborhood, the scene of his childhood. His train was delayed. His grandfather, who was also a preacher, undertook the sermon. After the grandfather had gone along a while Spurgeon appeared, and his grandfather said as he came down the aisle, "Charles is a better preacher than I, but he has not a better gospel to preach." I think we all might be greatly heartened in that awareness.

And for those of you who are setting out upon this high adventure, I can confidently say to you that the way does grow brighter as the days come and go, for there are gifts and endowments which belong each in its own turn to the various stages and periods of our discipleship. In the earlier years there is a vision which belongs to you. The young are highly hopeful and greatly envisioned and full of energy. There is an eagerness and an adventuresomeness which belong to that period. As we go along, we discover that, as the Lord gives and takes away, something deeper comes upon us. You will discover in the years that lie ahead a deepening of meaning in your days and a closer communication with God. So, I wish you every blessing as you set out upon the high road.

Let us ponder the name of the Savior. Someone has commented, and perhaps this does not do too well on a seminary campus, that there can be sometimes perhaps too much of an attempt to explain the Savior. His people ought to revere and adore and admire the Savior. I want to proceed upon that. I recognize that in taking the name of the Savior, Jesus Christ, we have a subject far beyond the power of any creature, or the Christian church itself in all its centuries, ever to exhaust. We can scarcely ever do more, after a lifetime of preaching and pondering our Lord, than touch the outer edge of the garment of his greatness and of his dearness.

Let me read these words from the first chapter of the Gospel according to John:

> *In the beginning was the Word, and the Word was with God, and the Word was God. The same was in the beginning with God. All things were made by him; and without him was not anything made that was made. In him was life; and the life was the light of men. And the light shineth in the darkness; and the darkness comprehended it not. There was a man sent from God, whose name was John. The same came for a witness, to bear witness of the Light, that all through him might believe. He was not that Light, but was sent to bear witness of that Light. That was the true Light, which lighteth every man that cometh into the world. He was in the world, and the world was made by him, and the world knew him not. He came unto his own, and his own received him not. But as many as received him, to them he gave power to become the sons of God, even to them that believe on his name: which were born, not of blood, nor of the will of the flesh, nor of the will of man, but of God. And the Word was made flesh, and dwelt among us, (and we beheld his glory, the glory as of the only begotten of the Father,) full of grace and truth. John bare witness of him, and cried, saying, This was he of whom I spake, He that cometh after me is preferred before me: for he was before me. And of his fullness have all we received, and grace for grace. For the law was given by Moses, but grace and truth came by Jesus Christ.*

What a vast subject! For all these nineteen hundred years the church has been dealing centrally with its Savior and with that great name, Jesus Christ. We shall never be able to exhaust the meaning of his name. And, yet, it is the agony and the ecstasy of our calling to try.

So we take that word *Jesus,* "and his name shall be called Jesus." That hitches him to us. The glory of our faith is that it is of the earth, earthy. In lands that do not know a large faith in Jesus Christ, such as India, Christian people make much of this, and rightly. They remind us that our faith centers in no far-off mystery. It is of flesh and blood. This is a glory of our faith. Our Lord lived here. He knew the context of our humanity. We may take great heart when we hear that lonely, terrible lament from Calvary, "I thirst." It ties him to our humanity. I do not know how one could approach a God who has no sense of our humanity. This is the glory of the New Testament. Jesus lived here! He said once to people, to his friends about a crowd of people, "I will not send them away hungry." Does that mean then that he knew what hunger was about? That he felt our cold and knew our heat? Experienced our sorrow and tasted our joy? This is the glory of our faith. "His name shall be called Jesus."

And for those people who try to remove the faith from the actualities of life, his name ought ever to reprove them and to bring them to the awareness that it was here, in the midst of our mud and dirt and glory and grandeur, that our faith was worked out. Our Lord's first confrontation, George Buttrick pointed out some years ago, as did Vernon Johns, was with deep structures of "gone wrongness," the great corporate evils of society which occurred among his own people. When he came back to Nazareth and entered the synagogue and opened the Book, he spoke those gracious words from the book of Isaiah. Their hearts must have leaped and light must have come into their eyes, as they recognized that this was one of their own. "The Spirit of the Lord is upon me," but when he dared to say to them that one of the prophets, Elijah, had not been sent to a widow of Israel, but to a Gentile widow from the town of Sarepta, a heathen community, their first enthusiasm chilled. Jesus was not content to leave it with that. He stated that in the days of another, Elisha, there were many lepers in Israel and not one of them was healed, but the Arab, Naaman, was healed. Their lovely response to the gracious words of the Scriptures suddenly turned to hostility. It was the evil of racism in his own people which first alienated Jesus from the people of the town of his upbringing.

It was in the earth that our faith was worked out. We must never forget it. The faith will never mean anything until it means something in the actual context of our daily problems. The problems of New York. The problems of wherever! This is what the faith is all about, and to separate it from that is to separate it from its source and from its sustenance.

There is another name which we use regularly, "Christ," the anointed of the Lord, and such he is. He fulfills the ancient Israelite trinity of prophet, priest, and king. He was a true prophet, for he spoke the perfect will of God, unmarred and unalloyed by any self-seeking motives, as all of the true prophets had done and as all true preaching must do. As priest, he offered the perfect sacrifice, his own body, for he went once and for all to be offered on the altar. As king, he reigns in majesty.

He is Divinity! Now, there is no Christian faith without that. It is a leap of faith beyond the power of reason to explain, but we discover in our discipleship that reason at least confirms what faith declares. Jesus Christ, the Lord! One cannot explain that, and one realizes that it is a part of the grand and creative torture of theological reflection in each new generation and in each new circumstance to try to make that title, Jesus Christ, clear. On one side, Jesus, and, as we repeat the Creed, we see our Lord's connection to the earth, to us. "Born of the Virgin Mary, suffered under Pontius Pilate." (That fixes a date for the faith.) "Was dead, buried." There is more than that. The early Christian people wrestled with this, and they came forth with the words "very man of very man" and "very God of very God."

When James Denny did his monumental work in 1908 on the person of Jesus, he made the comment that Matthew fixes the genealogy of our Lord in terms of his Jewishness. Luke does it in terms of his humanity. He traces our Lord back to the earliest mortal. John sets him in eternity. "In the beginning was the Word, and the Word was with God." Now this is a mystery. But any preacher who is not willing to confront and to acknowledge and to live in the grandeur and glory of this mystery will never preach the gospel. When Denny did that work, W. Robertson Nicoll wrote to him and said that he did not think that Denny was explicating sufficiently the divinity of our Lord. He said to Denny that he wanted to see a little clearer that Denny looked upon our Lord not only as the Son of God but also as God the

Son. That is the final mystery of faith. I must confess to you that in my earliest years I did not grasp that. I did not accept that. I did not surrender to that as I do now. As the years have come and gone, this has become an ever more precious truth in my life. He is not only the Son of God; he is God the Son.

The New Testament seeks again and again to assert that in this way or that. There is a grand bringing together of what was human and what was divine in him. Again and again these two aspects of our Lord's nature are brought together. Alexander Maclaren has pointed out, for instance, that he is born in a humble manger, but angels attend the birth and sing their songs of welcome if people will not. As a human, he sits wearied at the side of a well and asks for water. But as something more than a human, he gives to the woman water that satisfies forever. As a human, he sleeps wearily in the bow of the little fishing boat, but as something more than human, he stills the storm in the waters or the storm in the hearts of those who are with him. As a human, he weeps at the grave of Lazarus, but as something more than human, his voice reaches into the deep entrails of the grave, and the Gospels declare that the sheeted dead come forth. And so ever together must we hold these, Jesus Christ. No preaching is adequate that does not constantly, openly, explicitly deal with this central, glorious, grand mystery of the faith.

I have seen in this life many signs of the great power of Jesus Christ. Years ago, I was in the south of India. I had been in Calcutta and Delhi, but I had never been in the South Indian backwaters. One man, deeply touched by the Spirit of the Lord and seeking to relieve some of the unspeakable poverty of that old and almost instinctively religious land, suggested that I go with some others by boat, ten miles across a lake to a remote village. We set out through a canal of the backwaters and then out into the open lake. Finally, there was no sight of land anywhere. After ten miles, we came upon a little community of people. They live upon land literally not larger than a football stadium. For years, the water they drink has been polluted by pesticides, and, almost too horrible to speak, it is the same water in which they have washed and so forth.

But there is a church of Jesus Christ in that remote backwater settlement. Ten miles from any other human contact and on that sliver of land a little church, on top of it is a cross, representing the cross of Jesus Christ. Under that cross young Indian men had gone out ten miles by water to start for these people a new life. Under that cross, they had built a little community center, something new and wonderful for that remote community. Underneath that cross, they had begun teaching rope making and basket weaving, and under that cross they have led those people to protest and to confront an indifferent government about their own lack of water. And under that cross, a new sense of life has begun. I saw all of that, and late in the afternoon the people of that remote village, their children sitting in the front places, the adults and then the oldest of their people came together, and they sang in their own language some words which were interpreted for me as they sang. You know what they were? In their simple way they sang "Jesus is the Lord. He will not leave us. Though our fathers and our mothers leave, he will not leave us. Jesus is the Lord, and when we die he will not leave us. Jesus is the Lord." Under the cross, they have found his name, Jesus Christ, to be precious.

You and I will find it in all of the risings and fallings and shifting and changing scenes of our own existence. No one will ever fully preach that name. That is the glory of our calling, but that name will get ever brighter and ever more glorious as we seek to preach it, and when we come at last to the gates of eternal life, we will only then begin to understand that theme of the God-man, "the man for others" set down in the New Testament. And so, God has given him a name which is highly exalted. A name above every name. That at the name of Jesus every knee must at last bow and every tongue confess. I think only then will we begin to see the glory of the Lord whose we are, the winsome wonder of our Lord, Jesus Christ.

❦ 33 ❧

A Personal Word at Evening for Ministers and Others

Revelation 5:1–9

I want to read from the fifth chapter of the book of Revelation. Someone has commented that a strange thing about the Scriptures is that the most puzzling book of the Bible would be called the book of Revelation. And yet, in the midst of all that is cryptic about it and bewildering, mystifying, it has, here and yonder, thrusts which become deeply meaningful to those who approach this book with an openness of heart. I read from the fifth chapter of the book of Revelation, beginning at the first verse and continuing through the ninth verse:

> And I saw in the right hand of him that sat on the throne a book written within and on the backside, sealed with seven seals. And I saw a strong angel proclaiming with a loud voice, Who is worthy to open the book and to loose the seals thereof? And no man in heaven, nor on earth, neither under the earth, was able to open the book, neither to look thereon. And I wept much, because no man was found worthy to open and to read the book, neither to look thereon. And one of the elders saith unto me, Weep not: behold, the Lion of the tribe of Judah, the Root of David, hath prevailed to open the book, and to loose the seven seals thereof. And I beheld and lo, in the midst of the throne and of the four beasts, and in the midst of the elders, stood a Lamb as it had been slain, having seven arms and seven eyes, which are the seven spirits of God sent forth into all the earth. And he came and took the book out of the right hand of him that sat upon the throne. And when he had taken the book, the four beasts and four and twenty elders fell down before the Lamb, having every one of them harps, and golden vials full of odors, which are the prayers of saints. And they sung a new song,

---

Sermon delivered February 1, 1978. This sermon is not from National Radio Pulpit, but it is my legacy to those who come after me. It was preached at Trinity Lutheran Theological Seminary, Columbus, Ohio, and at Southern Baptist Theological Seminary, Louisville, Kentucky. —*GCT*

*saying, Thou art worthy to take the book and to open the seals
thereof: for thou wast slain, and has redeemed us to God by thy
blood out of every kindred, and tongue, and people, and nation.*

I want to probe in an informal way on discovering our authenticity, or our authority. I suppose there has never been anyone who has felt the pressure upon him or her to utter the word of God in any form of proclamation of the Word or in some other aspect of the church's work who has not at the same time deeply yearned to have a sense of authority and authenticity in the declaration of the living Word of God. I suppose that there would not be a single person who would not say that this has been a burning aspiration, a deep desire, and I suppose a part of that possesses its own selfishness. But this is a part of our humanity, and this is the stuff in which God has chosen to work. We are the projects of God. There is in us this desire, this yearning to be effective, to have authority, to have authenticity. We are likely to feel at one time or the other that such comes by some external manner, either by some art which conceals art, or what have you, or by some particular attractiveness of personality. There are people, I see them now and again on television, whose every gesture seems so measured and so planned. That may well be a form of authority, but I think anyone who looks at all deeply into the truth of the utterance of the gospel will discover that whatever authenticity we are to have lies beneath externals and may very well be apart from them.

How does one come to authority and power? One of the vivid memories of my childhood in the Louisiana swamp country is that of hearing the old black preachers expatiate loftily and magnificently upon this very passage. They made us yonder in the bayou country almost see the vivid imagery of the book of Revelation as they took it and made it their own. They spoke of this mysterious volume which had some vast significance and which had something to do in the cryptic language of the book of Revelation with the ending of the reign of Satan and the inauguration of the full authority of the kingdom of God and the redemption of the people of the earth.

They made us almost see this angelic courier moving through the heavenly places looking for someone to open the book, and I remember that they dealt with how the angel searched throughout the heavens, but no one was found worthy. Then they went on to say that the angel was dispatched to the earth and searched through the ends of the earthly creation for someone to break the seals and to reveal the deepest mysteries and by so doing to bring to an end the reign of Satan, but no one was found worthy. Then, as if perhaps being able to find someone in the nether world, the angel was dispatched into the regions of hell. What a vivid imagination that was! But in the regions of hell, no one was found worthy. They would then pause and speak of the weeping of the observer. The anguish of heart of someone wanting the seals to be broken and the mystery to be laid bare and the redemption to be consummated. "I wept much," said the writer, because no one was found worthy, and then there is a glorious deliverance as the angel says, "Weep not. I beheld, and, lo, in the midst of the throne and of the four beasts, in the midst of the elders, stood a Lamb as it had been slain. He came and took the book out of the right hand of him that sat on the throne. And when he had taken the book, they sang a new song, Thou art worthy to take the book, and to open the seals thereof: for thou wast slain." So that somewhere in the wounds of the hands also resided the power to open the book.

You and I will not want to court being hurt, and there are many people in the area of religion who hold back from exposing themselves to hurt. I have known pastors who have not allowed themselves to be true shepherds to their people because they wanted to insulate themselves and to protect themselves against being hurt and wounded. One hears that, now and again, among those who are supposedly very wonderful people who say, "I don't want to get hurt." So we stay out of things in which we ought to be involved. We move along on the fringes of life's busy and urgent matters because we want to protect ourselves. But there is a word here to be spoken which says that any authenticity that we are going to have as persons of faith and any authority that we are going to have as witnesses to the gospel of Jesus Christ will come because of our exposure to bruises and scars. There is no other way to authenticity. There is a certain counterfeit pose that one may maintain, but as to an entrance into the full, the true authority, into the glorious liberty of the sons of God, that comes by exposure and by wounds. There is no other way. If one looks back at those who have deeply affected their generation, the discovery will be made that almost without exception they did it against some minus, some ache, some pain in their own lives. I could run through the list.

This has surely been true of notable preachers of the gospel. Frederick Robertson in Brighton was so shy and so sensitive, together with a physical ailment, that he periodically considered giving up the work of the ministry. Yet, his ministry at Trinity Chapel in Brighton has been considered to be easily among the most iridescent, the most telling ministries in all of England in the nineteenth century. Alexander Maclaren, so honored among Baptists and others, was so shy that his biographer said he could hardly speak to a servant girl about her salvation. He did his work all of those long years at Union Chapel in Manchester up against that kind of shyness. Charles Spurgeon suffered such rheumatic pains that he was out of London for almost all of the London preaching season every year. You may go through the list. Joseph Parker at City Temple seemed to have an endless need to be congratulated. It was a sign of a certain insecurity deep within his personality. Of course, every Christian minister ought to learn to say, to think at least, what Frederick Robertson is reported to have said to a woman who gushed, "Rector, that was a magnificent sermon." His reply was, "Thank you, madam. The devil has already told me so."

The pulpit of the twentieth century will know no brighter figure than Harry Emerson Fosdick. All over this country, even in the deepest sections of conservative enclaves, one hears his hymn "God of Grace and God of Glory." His years at the Riverside Church were among the brightest chronicles of Protestantism in this century. Dr. Fosdick spent three months in an Elmira institution with a complete nervous breakdown, and he himself said that without the harrowing experience of that breakdown, he never would have written *The Meaning of Prayer*, which has addressed so many people in so many parts of the earth. Martin Luther King, who may have been the only authentic saint ever produced in this country, was a dear friend of mine. We vacationed together often, and even in his lightest moments there was about him a certain brooding. One could almost call it a melancholy. He did his work against that. George Truett, who charmed the American South in the first half of the twentieth century, did his pulpit work under the shadow of the memory of a hunting accident in which his dearest friend was accidentally killed by Truett's gun. One of the most notable and gifted preachers of our generation once said to me in an anguish that he always had to live with a deep sense of worthlessness.

At some time, who can say when, there will be a crown of thorns pressed down upon your head. It may be some private anguish. It may be some profoundly disturbing condition in your own family. One cannot detail the direction whence the affliction will come, but when it does, you will have every right to rail against it and to cry out against that kind of providence, even to argue with God, to withstand him to the face. There is a large place for that in true faith. It is an artificial, it is a pretended faith that cannot, at any time, contend with the Eternal. "He knows our frame, he remembers that we are dust." If you want to cry out against that solemn appointment whenever it comes to you, do so. But do one other thing. Take it. Accept. For was it not our Lord's word that the cup he looked into, the awful agony which waited for him, did not come from unfriendly hands: "The cup which my Father hath given, shall I not drink of it?" I promise you this, if you can take whatever deep hurt that occurs in your life and hold it up before God and say to him, even in bitterness, of this which you despise and this which you hate, "If there is anything you can do with it, take it, and use it." I promise you, you will be utterly amazed at what will occur. For what is being said here in this passage is that our Lord himself to come to saviorhood had to come by the way of suffering.

That strange book of Hebrews with all of its daring assertions says more, that the captain of our salvation was, one almost hesitates to quote it, perfected to saviorhood by suffering. "Though he were a son, yet he learned obedience by the things which he suffered." What a strange and cryptic word, but how instructive for us! Such will surely occur. How you will deal with it is another matter. If it is offered to the Lord, it becomes a powerful and moving and authoritative factor in your ministry. If it is avoided, then your ministry ends in shallows.

What is at the heart of our faith? It is a cross. Not a cross of roses. It is not a sweet cross, but a bitter one. Our Lord himself, to come to the fulfillment, to the fullness of saviorhood traveled by the way of Nazareth, in those lost eighteen years save for one relatively minor incident, apparently, by the way of Galilee and by the way of Jerusalem, but what made him our Savior happened on a hill outside the city's gates. He met all that hell and perverted people and wicked and fallen institutions of government and church could do to him. It was in his accepting of what looked like a terrible and tragic and pointless suffering that he came to saviorhood. One goes in imagination to Bethlehem, hearing the angels sing, and the heart is moved. One sees him again in the temple at twelve, foreshadowing his own years of ministry. Follow him through the villages of Galilee, and we are moved. Hear him arguing with those who will not see his larger sense of God. Watch him committing to his own fellowship, to the community of faith, the tools of discipleship which he came to give, and we are touched by all that. But, my God! when we come to Calvary, more than our minds is affected. Something beyond the power to describe occurs. It is there that he becomes, in truth, savior.

If you and I are going to enter fellowship with him, we must enter it by the way of the fellowship of his sufferings. So! Whenever it happens, that coronation of thorns, take it. How do you get through it? How do you manage? How do you carry on? How do you go before people to deal with them when your own heart is breaking? And how do you sustain it across all of the years that those of you who are young will be called upon to do your work?

Let me share a personal experience. I graduated from Oberlin Seminary in 1940. I know that seems so ancient to some of you. The spring of my senior year, the *Christian Century* sent a letter to all of us who were graduating. It was really a plea for subscriptions, but it was a touching letter done in the inimitable language of Charles Clayton Morrison, then editor of the *Century*. That letter referred to our leaving seminary, and it spoke of how we would soon be leaving the insights of the seminary, leaving with an eagerness and an enthusiasm. "What will you do?" Then it quoted a word from Wordsworth, what will you do when your ministry "fades into the light of common day"? It was about the bruises and the long stretch. Well, the days of my seminary were great days for me, as yours are for you. And those dear people who led me and the rest of my colleagues into the deep things of our faith are almost all gone. They were great names in those days — Walter Marshall Horton, Clarence Tucker Craig, Thomas Graham, Francis Buckler, Herbert Gordon May — but we were leaving all that, and now how many years have gone? Nearly sixty.

Long since I have lost that initial enthusiasm, and my ministry has long since "faded into the light of common day." I have kept no record. I have no notion of how many pulpits I've gone in and come out of. I hardly remember the ends of the earth to which my preaching has carried me. I do know that sometimes I have come out of pulpits so spent that I wished to God that I never had to go into another. But I can promise you this! That every time that happens something else will happen. Every time you're bruised and hurt, if you will but seek to be faithful, something else will occur. How shall I explain that other? Perhaps I can best do it in some lines from a spiritual of my own people which most of you will have heard. You remember that haunting, lovely spiritual, "There is a balm in Gilead to make the wounded whole." Then the verse "Sometimes I feel discouraged and think my work's in vain, but then the Holy Spirit revives my soul again." Whatever bruises and hurts there are ahead of you, I can promise you that.

ISBN 0-8170-1339-3

9 780817 013394